*The lights in the White House
burned late the night before...*

Five Days to War

April 2-6, 1917

FIVE DAYS TO WAR

April 2-6, 1917

by Ernest R. Dupuy

A Giniger Book

published in association with

STACKPOLE BOOKS

First Edition
April 1967

DESIGNED BY HAROLD FRANKLIN

This is an impressionistic mosaic of America's entry into war in 1917. It is based on research colored by my own memories as a then young New York National Guard officer who expected a commission in Teddy Roosevelt's dream division, and who, as a reporter on the New York *Herald,* witnessed part of the drama and interviewed not a few of the principal personalities engaged.

To my wife, Laura Nevitt Dupuy, who, with our year-old son, shared that experience with me and ninety-two million other Americans, goes my heartfelt appreciation of her keen recollection and invaluable assistance in planning and composing the mosaic.

The Historical Evaluation and Research Organization of Washington, D.C., and, in particular, its staffer, Linnea Raine, assiduously combed the files of the contemporary press.

Mrs. Estelle Campbell's sense of pictorial news values has contributed greatly to the quality and scope of the illustrations.

Finally, the canny suggestions and meticulous guidance of my publisher friend, K. S. Giniger, have been of tremendous aid.

R. ERNEST DUPUY

Arlington, Virginia

CONTENTS

PROLOGUE:

A Nice Place to Live

PROLOGUE:

A Nice Place to Live

THE AMERICANS OF 1917 thought of their country as "a nice place to live." But the United States was reaching the end of an era. The Gay Nineties had slipped away, yet the age of automation was still a dream. There were no electric razors, no "do-it-yourself" gimmicks, no radio broadcasting or television. The antimacassar and the spittoon had deserted the living room, but the phonograph was a family standby.

There was plenty to do and to see and to enjoy. Some people cruised on yachts, others hired rowboats at a quarter an hour. In the season, the beaches at seashore and lake were crowded. *Bon vivants* were looking askance at the encroachments of the Prohibitionists — a Constitutional amendment that would bar strong liquor was actually before the individual states for ratification—but most people never gave the matter a thought. The rich opened champagne; the poor "rushed the growler" for beer at the corner saloon.

It was an era of sharp contrasts, too, particularly in New York. Financier J. Pierpont Morgan, Jr., might prefer the haughty atmosphere of the New York Yacht Club or Delmonico's, but Jack's and Shanley's were favorite spots for another financier. This individual, a man of gargantuan appetite, had but recently richly endowed Johns Hopkins University. He was James Buchanan Brady, better known as "Diamond Jim."

The theater was thriving. U-boat warfare had sent producer

Life in America in 1917
was simple and uncomplicated.
Along New York's fashionable Fifth Avenue,
the mood was unhurried.

*While the corner saloon and the "growler" of beer were
the setting and taste of the poor, champagne, caviar,
and the posh atmosphere of Delmonico's, Shanley's,
the New York Yacht Club, or Jack's for bon vivants
and financiers, were more in keeping with their
cultivated pocketbooks and tastes. The speakeasy
was yet to come. Prohibition, as a constitutional
amendment, was already before the individual states for
ratification. But, in 1917, few people gave the matter a thought.*

Charles Frohman to his death in the *Lusitania,* but David Belasco and
the Shuberts were producing a succession of hits, while Florenz Ziegfeld
was, as he said, "glorifying the American girl" in his annual Follies. A
new playwright named Eugene O'Neill had joined the Provincetown
Players. And, on the lighter side, vaudeville was still at the apex of its
popularity.

In New York the Metropolitan Opera House was always crowded.
But all over the nation people were also crowding into little movie
houses—an estimated 10,000 of them existed—where one could gulp in
the thrills of *The Perils of Pauline,* the gun-toting exploits of William
S. Hart and Tom Mix, the shockingly sinuous curves of the first "vamp,"

Theda Bara, or the uproarious slapstick of Mack Sennett's Keystone Cops.

The era was one of humor. People could laugh, and stars of stage and screen gave them belly-laughs aplenty: Charlie Chaplin, Al Jolson, Eddie Cantor, W. C. Fields and Fanny Brice; the homespun humor of lariat-twirling Will Rogers; the side-splitting antics of Laurel and Hardy, of Buster Keaton and Harold Lloyd.

Motion-picture actors were gaining in stature: Mary Pickford, America's darling; the Gish sisters, Lillian and Dorothy; Gloria Swanson; Greta Garbo; to say nothing of patent-leather-haired Rudolph Valentino, who tickled feminine sensibilities. As for Douglas Fairbanks, he had already won his spurs on the legitimate stage.

It was a reading nation, too. Writers Frank Norris, Upton Sinclair, Booth Tarkington and Winston Churchill (no relative of Britain's rising

Music's mecca in America has always been the Metropolitan Opera. In 1917, as today, there was standing room only. Tails and evening dress were de rigeur. And it was possibly only at the "Met," that the "Four Hundred" ever rubbed shoulders with would-be society and immigrant alike. It was one of the golden years of the Met's history. Voices like Caruso, Hempel, Amato, Bori, Ferrar, Scotti, Galli-Curci filled the great red and gold auditorium.

Charlie Chaplin
personified
an era
of good humor.

(Right) *She was
"America's Darling."
She was that naive,
wholesome, embodiment of
everyone's dream girl,
the kid sister,
the girl next door,
the sweetheart,
the future wife.
Her name was Mary Pickford*

young politician) were popular, as was Jack London. And, in a species of delayed action, Theodore Dreiser's *Sister Carrie,* in its third edition, suddenly became a best seller.

Factories were humming, for munitions-making for the Allies had become big business. But Detroit, in particular, was remarkable for what had become a national industry—the making of automobiles. It was the era of the Stutz Bearcat and the Marmon, but above all, it was the era of Henry Ford's "tin Lizzy." Vanderbilt Cup races on Long Island attracted people in droves, as did the grueling 24-hour grinds at the old Sheepshead Bay racetrack. Speed was the magnet of attention.

On the East Coast, shipyards were busy
on an overtime basis replacing Allied
vessels being sunk by German U-boat
torpedoes. At Staten Island, where these
ship builders are seen leaving the yard,
they were already working on a double shift.

One daredevil driver, a man named Edward V. Rickenbacker, had actually driven 134 miles an hour at Florida's Daytona Beach, breaking the world record.

In the cities, the police who tried to control the waxing automobile traffic had discarded horses and bicycles for motors, had thrown their classic dome-shaped helmets in the discard in favor of snappy caps. The words and music of "In My Merry Oldsmobile" had supplanted the semiscornful, semi-envious "Get Out and Get Under," while the street urchin's cry of "Get a Horse!" was becoming passé. But outside

"Who do you think you are, Eddie Rickenbacker?"
Speed was America's mania. Edward Rickenbacker
was a daredevil driver. In 1917, he sped
134 miles per hour at Florida's Daytona Beach
to smash the world record.
The automobile was here to stay.

the urban neighborhoods country roads were atrocious, and the nation's reliance for long-distance travel was on the vast railroad network linking the big cities, while the ubiquitous trolley car clanged and pounded through both city and suburb.

Telephones in private houses were still comparatively few. The telegraph was here, of course, and—until England in 1914 cut the German link—the Old and the New World were closely coupled by cable.

Wireless telegraphy had emerged from its experimental stage to prove its usefulness in maritime life-saving. A number of enthusiastic amateurs who dubbed themselves "hams" were actually outstripping the professionals in long-range contacts. German money and German technicians had constructed two transatlantic wireless stations, one at Sayville, Long Island, the other at Amityville, Long Island, to span the Atlantic in place of the lost cable link. But the wireless was still not a totally accepted commercial communications medium. Voice broadcasting, except for a few experimental plants, did not exist.

Women's suffrage was a burning issue. Its battling protagonists, women such as Mrs. Carrie Chapman Catt, Mrs. August Belmont, Mrs. Harriot Stanton Blatch and the comely Inez Mulholland were making speeches and leading parades across the country.

Baseball was the national obsession, with "Take Me Out to the Ball Game" its theme song. The major league teams were in Spring training down South, while, in car-barns all over the nation, workmen were furbishing up the open-air trolley cars that would carry the fans to the ball parks when the season opened.

Taken all in all, the United States *was* a nice place to live. Patriotism was still a nice word. Americans were a simple people, with simple objectives and simple directness. They were people who collectively could and did thoroughly enjoy a Fourth of July oration, who

It was Spring and time for the open air trolleys
to be spruced up and put back on the tracks.
This Magazine Street car served New Orleans.
Baseball was in the air and trolleys were
the most popular form of transportation to the ball parks.

The war in Europe, by 1917, had divided the nation into two
schools of thought: pacifist and isolationist on one hand and
pro-preparedness and interventionist on the other. Both sides
sought to influence the nation through the press and by parades
of strength. In New York, there were many peace parades (above)
and demonstrations (below) requiring police protection.

could applaud a screaming eagle and who couldn't understand why the rest of the world didn't love their cantankerous isolationism and proselytizing ways. With comparatively few exceptions, they were convinced that any American could lick the world with one hand tied behind his back. So they spurned military preparedness for defense; William Jennings Bryan had spoken for most of them when he declared that in moment of need "a million Americans would spring to arms overnight."

Unfortunately, at this moment the United States was also a badly divided nation. The division began when the assassination of Archduke Francis Ferdinand of Austro-Hungary at Sarajevo, Serbia, on June 28, 1914, stirred thunderheads of war that burst August 1-4. The German invasion of Belgium brought a declaration of American neutrality from President Woodrow Wilson. Almost immediate encroachments by both Britain and Germany on the doctrine of freedom of the seas produced

Suffragettes rejoiced when President Wilson came out in favor of their cause. But woman's suffrage remained a stirring issue. Across the nation, women such as Mrs. Carrie Chapman Catt and Mrs. August Belmont led parades and made speeches seeking to win male votes to give American women the franchise.

During his first term, President Woodrow Wilson tried to mediate the war in Europe while keeping the United States neutral. He was re-elected to a second term, in 1916, with the slogan, "He kept us out of war."

On May 7, 1915, the Cunard liner Lusitania was torpedoed without warning by a German U-Boat in the North Atlantic. She sank with a loss of 1,198 men women and children including 124 Americans. This artist's rendering of the scene appeared in news papers and magazines of the time. The headline is from the New York Times.

intense irritation in the United States and contradictory sentiments of American sympathy with individual belligerents. Superior British surface sea power, strangulating the Central Powers, brought unrestricted submarine retaliation by Germany, straining American neutrality. The sinking of the Cunard liner *Lusitania* without warning, May 7, 1915—which resulted in the drowning of 1,198 men, women and children, including 124 Americans—as callously as a handyman might drown a litter of unwanted kittens, brought a wave of revulsion against Germany in the United States.

President Wilson's statement at that time that "there is such a thing as a man being too proud to fight" was repudiated by many Americans. But his three sharp notes to the German government—the

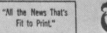

The New York Times.

EXTRA
5:30 A. M.

VOL. LXIV. NO. 20,925. ..... NEW YORK, SATURDAY, MAY 8, 1915.—TWENTY-FOUR PAGES. ONE CENT

LUSITANIA SUNK BY A SUBMARINE, PROBABLY 1,260 DEAD; TWICE TORPEDOED OFF IRISH COAST; SINKS IN 15 MINUTES; CAPT. TURNER SAVED, FROHMAN AND VANDERBILT MISSING; WASHINGTON BELIEVES THAT A GRAVE CRISIS IS AT HAND

Early in the morning, on July 30, 1916, New York City was rocked awake by a tremendous explosion. Black Tom Island, at Bayonne, N. J., a major shipping point for munitions to Europe in New York harbor, blew up. The detonation was so violent that bridges over the East River trembled and windows from the Battery to 42nd Street were shattered. Shrapnel bombarded lower Manhattan and shock waves from the blast were felt in Philadelphia and Baltimore.
The damage at Black Tom (above) was extensive and property loss set at $22 million. German sabotage was charged. But Black Tom was only the first of many disasters such as those (below and above right)
which were to be attributed to enemy agents and sabotage.

last of them a virtual ultimatum—got action. Germany announced that henceforth no vessel would be sunk without proper warning.

Tension in the United States lessened for a time, but it rose again as German sabotage of American installations serving Allied armament needs was revealed. The Black Tom explosion in New York harbor, July 30, 1916, rocked the city and caused a property loss of twenty-two million dollars. The wrecking on January 11, 1917, of the Canadian Car & Foundry plant at Kingsland, New Jersey, aroused further indignation. In consequence, the Austrian ambassador, Dr. Constantin Dumba, and the German military and naval attachés, Captains Franz von Papen and Carl von Boy-Ed, who were all involved in the sabotage, were declared *persona non grata* and expelled.

Meanwhile, President Wilson's efforts to maintain a neutral course had been rewarded by the American people. He was reelected in November, 1916, on the slogan "He kept us out of war."

In January, 1917, German civilian and military leaders agreed that to attain success, unrestricted submarine warfare must be resumed at once, thus reducing Britain to starvation. The war, they concluded,

(Above) *A series of blasts in American armament factories in 1916 and 1917 resulted in charges of sabotage leveled at Germany's military attaché, Captain Franz von Papen. He was ordered expelled.*

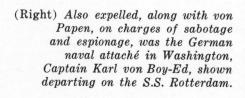

(Right) *Also expelled, along with von Papen, on charges of sabotage and espionage, was the German naval attaché in Washington, Captain Karl von Boy-Ed, shown departing on the S.S. Rotterdam.*

could then be ended before any American intervention could succeed. German Ambassador Count Johann von Bernstorff officially notified the U.S. Secretary of State of the German intentions. February 1 was the target date. Under humiliating conditions, one American ship per week would be permitted to sail into British waters.

President Wilson, addressing a joint session of the Congress on February 3, announced the breaking of diplomatic relations with Germany. Von Bernstorff was sent packing, but the President's request to Congress to put guns and Navy gun crews on American merchantmen was stymied by a filibuster in the Senate led by Senator Robert M. La Follette of Wisconsin. When the Congress adjourned without action, Wilson armed the merchantmen anyway, by executive order.

On March 1 an intercepted and deciphered memorandum from German Foreign Secretary Alfred Zimmermann to the German minister to Mexico, Heinrich von Eckhardt, offering alliance with the Mexican

After a hiatus of nine months, Germany, in February, 1917, resumed unrestricted submarine warfare against ships at sea. The German military were convinced they could starve Britain into submission before the United States would intervene and join the Allied cause.

government should war break out between Germany and the United States and adding "it is understood that Mexico is to reconquer the lost territory in New Mexico, Texas and Arizona," was published in the United States. It aroused tremendous resentment; its added injunction that Mexico solicit the aid of Japan crystallized public opinion for the first time along the Pacific coast.

American public opinion, as the war abroad had dragged on, had hardened into three distinct segments: vehement advocates of war with Germany, conservative-minded people opposed in principle to war but also jealous of national honor, and pacifists, divided in motive but united in objective to keep the United States from making war on Germany.

In prewar years, German Ambassador to the United States, Count Johann von Bernstorff, was the darling of Washington's social set. He had a military bearing, a red mustache and he epitomized the German aristocrat. As the European war dragged on, however, his popularity waned until, with President Wilson's breaking of diplomatic relations with Germany on Feb. 3, 1917, he was asked to leave.

LYING IN WAIT

UNTER DER OCEAN STRASSE

PEACE AVE

A typical newspaper cartoon of the time commenting on Germany's resumption of unrestricted submarine warfare. The Kaiser, wearing a mailed glove with a U-boat as a club, is about to clobber Uncle Sam.

Soon after America's entry into the war with Germany,
William Randolph Hearst was photographed
with his wife and five sons in uniform.

The tumult and the shouting were stimulated by propaganda, most of which was disseminated through the medium of the daily press. Americans were justly proud of their free-wheeling press. In consequence, although carefully documented news was frequently dismissed as "newspaper talk," in general the country lapped up the pabulum of partisan editorial policy.

Allied propaganda astutely pointed its appeal to American humanitarian instincts. The propaganda of the Central Powers was heavy, stilted, frequently irritating. Much of its effect was negated by the German sabotage campaign.

Preaching the only sane policy for America to follow was one of neutrality, Joseph Medill McCormick, of the family which published the Chicago Tribune, was an outspoken Anglophobe.

Herman Ridder, publisher of the New Yorker Staats-Zeitung *was one of many German-American newspaper publishers throughout the land supporting the German cause on the eve of the war declaration.*

James Gordon Bennett's New York *Herald,* its sister sheet the *Evening Telegram* and his dilettante Paris *Herald* all moved editorially to the Allied cause. William Randolph Hearst, whose chain of newspapers spanned the continent from New York to San Francisco, together with Joseph Medill McCormick and his family's Chicago *Tribune,* fostered the unreasoning Anglophobia of Irish-Americans ridden by age-old hatreds and exasperated by Britain's drastic suppression of the Irish Easter Monday Revolt in 1916. The younger McCormick brother, Colonel Robert R. "Bertie," was already grooming his National Guard artillery regiment for active service. Herman Ridder's *New Yorker Staats-Zeitung* not unnaturally headed a score of German-American newspapers throughout the country in supporting the German cause.

The New York *Call,* organ of the anti-war Socialist Labor Party, and the *Jewish Daily Forward,* whose Yiddish-set columns were pored over on New York's East Side by immigrants who had fled Imperial Russia's pogroms, both—for reasons radically divergent—pled the cause of people who wanted nothing to do with war.

Adding to the din were the influential voices of venerable "Marse Henry" Watterson, editor of the Louisville *Courier-Journal,* and the Emporia (Kansas) *Gazette's* William Allen White. Both men were sincere patriots, but they lived in an Anglo-Saxon world of stark black and white below billowing folds of red, white and blue bunting, a world that had no room for Hohenzollerns and Hapsburgs.

Such was the American scene and such the line-up of the American people when President Woodrow Wilson called the new Congress to a special session on April 2.

From the plains of America's midwest, William Allen White, publisher of the Emporia, Kansas, Gazette, called for war against Germany and an end to the houses of Hohenzollen and Hapsburg.

"Such was the American scene..."

*The peaceful mien of the White House was
soon to give way to the steadily
escalating tensions of war. But, for the moment
at least, the mood was quiet and unhurried.
It was the lull before the storm.*

President Woodrow Wilson and his cabinet at the time of the
declaration of war (front row, left to right) Secretary of Commerce William
C. Redfield, Secretary of State Robert Lansing, Secretary of Agriculture
David F. Houston, President Wilson, Secretary of the Treasury
William G. McAdoo, and Postmaster General Albert A. Burleson;
(second row, left to right) Secretary of the Navy Josephus Daniels, Secretary of
Labor W. B. Wilson, Secretary of War Newton D. Baker, Attorney General
Thomas W. Gregory, and Secretary of the Interior Franklin K. Lane.

*While the pacifists and interventionists paraded and orated in
their efforts to sway American public opinion about the war,
several young Pinehurst society matrons took action.
They organized themselves into the "Home Defense of Pinehurst
Association," and took weekly target practice at a local gun club.*

(Left) *As the war in Europe dragged on, Americans across the
nation divided into advocates of peace on the one hand
and advocates of preparedness on the other. These women are
about to lead one of the major peace marches through streets of New York.*

(Below) *While others marched, a women's volunteer motor corps
sprang into being in Boston. Said to be the only one of
its kind in the country, the unit was composed entirely of women,
"all skillful automobile drivers," according to the New York* Times.

(Left) *To counter the peace march publicity, preparedness parades
were also staged in New York. This one was led by* (left to right) *Thomas
Robins, Peter Cooper Hewitt, Thomas A. Edison and W. D. Saunders.*

(Above)
*Frances Alda
of the
Metropolitan Opera
starred as Columbia
in the tableau,
"Battle Cry of War"
at the Hippodrome.*

(Below) *Vicent Astor's yacht,*
Nourmahal, *which he loaned
to the government
for use in coastwise
anti-submarine defense.*

(Right) *John D. Rockefeller, Sr.
while vacationing at Daytona, Florida.*

(Below) *James Buchanan (Diamond Jim)
Brady decked out in all his finery.*

(Above) *While the nation debated peace or war, the Congress Street docks
in Brooklyn, New York, was the scene of a million dollar fire which
gutted twelve vessels and surrounding piers. The blaze was laid to sabotage.*
(Below) *On the West Coast, violence marred a preparedness day parade in
San Francisco where a bomb was thrown into a group of paraders.*

(Above) *The sabotaging of the Canadian Car and Foundry plant at Kingsland, N. J., led to the eventual expulsion of the Austrian Ambassador and the German military and naval attachés to the United States.*
(Below) *The resumption of unrestricted submarine warfare by Germany brought an end to American diplomatic relations with that country.*

*Women in all states were bitten by the preparedness bug. This group,
charging across the drill field of Governor's Island in
New York harbor, were members of the volunteer Women's Self Defense League.*

*"The Plattsburg Idea," conceived by Maj. Gen. Leonard Wood,
was put into action on Governor's Island where
Wood was in command. These new recruits to the
volunteer Officers Reserve Corps were drilled with dummy wooden guns.*

As the war clouds gathered over the United States,
police, vigilante groups and National Guard units took up posts
at bridges, railroad yards and other sensitive points to
prevent sabotage. This unit is changing the guard at a pier in New York Harbor.

THE FIRST DAY / *Part One*

"You Must Be Brutal and Ruthless..."

New York Tribune

First to Last — the Truth: News · Editorials · Advertisements

WEATHER
Colder, much colder by to-night. To-morrow partly over-cast and colder, with fresh south winds

Full Report on Page 4

CIRCULATION
Over 100,000 Daily
Net Paid, Non-Returnable

LXXVI No. 25,705 · Copyright 1917; The Tribune Ass'n · MONDAY, APRIL 2, 1917 · · · ONE CENT *In New York City*

00 Pacifists, aring Tulips, o Crusading

"atriotic Pilgrims" Will ave Them to Wash-gton This Morning

le Onslaught Upon the Capital

Party Armed with e Brassards, "Keep Out of War"

sand militant pacifists, each th a white tulip, left New k midnight for Washington...

Pacifists and Antis Both Are Forbidden To Hold Parades

Washington, April 1. Pacifists, mar-shalled by the Emergency Peace Federation...

'EST HE FORGET

Pacifist Sermon by Dr. Holmes Moves His Trustees to Act

Pastor Offers to Quit Church of the Messiah—Says No Order of President or Governor Will Force Him to Engage in War

The Rev. Dr. John Haynes Holmes, minister of the Church of the Messiah...

Berlin Fears U. S. Learned Of More Plots

Zimmermann's Mexican Plan Exposed Through Knowl-edge of "Inside" Code

Would Give Insight Into Other Secrets

Foreign Secretary's Defence Fails to Check Criticism for Being Found Out

Copenhagen, April 1. The German-Mexican alliance incident, it is evident...

U. S. Ambassador Leaves Austria; Break Is Denied

Vienna Says Penfield Will Re-turn—Washington Silent on Sudden Departure

Amsterdam, April 1. Telegraphing from Vienna, the correspondent of the semi-official "Norddeutsche Allgemeine Zeitung" of Berlin, says...

Rain Saves Crops In Middle West

Loss of Billions of Dollars Is Averted

St. Louis, April 1. Millions of dol-lars have been saved for the farmers...

Cunard Liners Arrive

Carpathia and Ascania Jour-ney Safely from Britain

The Cunard Line steamship Ascania and Carpathia, from British ports, ar-rived at Quarantine last night...

A Washington News Item

Washington, April 1. The War and Navy departments continued to-day...

Congress Ready to Declare State of War Now Exists; Country in Militant Mood

Most Crucial Session Since Civil War Begins at Noon To-day

Wilson Is Ready With War Message

Will Deliver Address After Both Houses Complete Organization

(By The Associated Press.)

Washington, April 1. Congress, called in extraordinary session by President Wilson, will meet to-morrow to determine the most important issues before that body since the Civil War...

Meet at Noon To-day

May Demand Strong Action

"Let Germany Do It"

By C. W. Gilbert

Washington, April 1. We shall know in a day or perhaps two day: whether it is the fault of democracy or the fault of President Wil-son. Down here at the capital you are as sured at every turn that it is the fault of democracy...

Europe's Pacifists Eagerly Awaiting Wilson's Address

Allies' Replies to Hollweg Also To Be Watched for Bearing on War's End

By ARTHUR S. DRAPER

London, April 1. Europe has come to the front again, and will be in the air until the warring nations are again locked in a death struggle...

Poll of 83 Representatives Shows Nation Is for Decisive Action

Pacifists Strong Only in the West

Majority Favors Universal Service, but Opposes Send-ing Army Abroad

(From The Tribune Bureau)

Washington, April 1. There is no doubt that a great majority of the 65th Congress will vote either for war with Germany, or for the declaration that a "state of war" exists, if and when the President asks for the ultimate measure...

Tribune's Questions And the Answers

Against Sending Troops Abroad

East and South Strongest for War

THE FIRST DAY/Part One

"You Must Be Brutal and Ruthless..."

MONDAY, APRIL 2, the first day of Holy Week in 1917, was an hour old. A haggard and sleepless man sat in the Presidential study of the White House in Washington. He was a man of enormous personal rectitude and impetuous self-will; a cadaverous combination of patriot and puritan. His name was Woodrow Wilson.

Outside, a cab slid under the portico out of the drizzle to disgorge a solitary passenger. A moment later, Frank Irving Cobb, editor in chief of the New York *World*, was ushered into the study, answering a hurry call. For Cobb was the only newspaperman the President really trusted, and Wilson had sought his solace.

At that moment, in the cold dawn waters off Ushant, three thousand miles away and five time-hours ahead, a battered lifeboat, some gratings and other flotsam bobbed together with several human bodies —mute evidence of the unwarned torpedoing of the freighter *Aztec*, the first American merchantman to carry guns and a Navy gun crew as protection against German U-boats.

The White House knew nothing yet of this latest evidence of Germany's resumption of unrestricted warfare. But Cobb, of course, knew of all that had happened since the German declaration of such warfare on January 31. He knew, too—for it was common knowledge now—that the President would address the new Congress in special session today, and that in all probability he would ask for a declaration of war.

Unburdening himself, the President told of the sleepless nights he had passed, going over the litany of his disappointments, his arid search to restore the peace he so ardently desired. Each time he found a loophole of escape from war, the German government had deliberately blocked it by some new outrage. Now, it seemed, there was no alternative to the declaration which he would later today ask of the Congress.

Cobb's consolatory comment that the President's hand had been forced did not satisfy Mr. Wilson. War, he told his listener, would mean the defeat of Germany and a dictated peace.

"It means an attempt to construct a peacetime civilization with war

Frank I. Cobb, editor-in-chief of the New York World,
*was the only newspaperman President Wilson wholly trusted.
Just after midnight, the day President Wilson was to go
before the Congress to ask for war with Germany,
Cobb was summoned to the White House to listen
to the President unburden himself
and discuss his long, fruitless quest
for an end to the European conflict.*

standards, and at the end of the war there will be no bystanders with
sufficient power to influence the terms. . . .

"Once lead this people into war," he continued, "and they'll forget there ever was such a thing as tolerance. To fight you must be brutal
and ruthless . . . and the spirit will enter into the very fibre of our national
life. . . ."

They talked until the dawn came and a solitary horse-drawn milk
wagon clop-clopped its leisurely way down Pennsylvania Avenue.

All over the United States people began getting up. Men struggled
into high choker collars, women lashed themselves into straight-front
corsets.

Their breakfasts finished, they began going about their lawful—or
unlawful—occasions. Most of their thoughts were concerned in one way
or another with the threat of coming war blazoned in the morning
papers, and some people were actually doing something about it. Up
at West Point on the Hudson, all 138 members of the U.S. Military
Academy's First (senior) Class—from Harris Jones of Connecticut, the
No. 1 man, to John Richard Nygaard of Wisconsin, the class "goat"—

*Little noted because of the strict censorship then in effect,
the American Line passenger ship, St. Louis, was among the first
to run the gauntlet of Germany's unilaterally imposed "Barred Zone."
Here the St. Louis, heavily armed both fore and aft, is depicted passing
the Statue of Liberty outward bound. The drawing was published in the
New York Times, Mid-Week Pictorial five days
after the ship's safe arrival at an undisclosed European port.*

were finding it difficult to keep their minds on the morning's recitations,
for speculation on early graduation was buzzing. Thus it had been in
all our previous wars, and no one today doubted the President's
intention.

In New York City, roustabouts and street cleaners were sweeping
up the refuse in the big temporary tabernacle at 168th Street and Broadway
where the Rev. Billy Sunday, one-time professional baseball player
turned evangelist, had the day before—Palm Sunday—inaugurated a
campaign to "drive out the devil that is in New York." Some twenty

thousand people, including many notables, had crowded into the structure then, and as many more had been turned away.

Guests in the Ritz-Carlton Hotel were interrupted in their perusal of the morning news when an agile pet monkey, escaping from his owners' suite, led a bellboy posse a merry chase through heavy-carpeted corridors. On West 50th Street, later in the forenoon, a truck driver, perhaps agitated by the day's headlines, dropped an empty packing case on a passerby. His reward was a black eye which the *Herald* termed "a pippin," but which cost the donor a five-dollar fine in West Side Court from a neutral magistrate.

Colonel Edward M. House was President Wilson's
close friend, political guide and confidant.
He was considered the most influential private citizen
in the United States during the Wilson administrations.
The President used Colonel House as his
personal emissary on a peace-seeking mission to Europe.

*The burning issue of women's suffrage had
its share of dynamic proponents—among them
Mrs. Carrie Chapman Catt shown here in a rare moment of repose.*

Down on Wall Street, the stock market began rallying from a war-scare flurry during which rails and U.S. Steel had taken appreciable drops.

Overseas, good news from the fronts was being digested and exploited in dispatches moving from London; Haig's armies were sweeping Saint-Quentin, while the French were breaking through "strong trench lines."

In Washington, by ten o'clock, the Government Printing Office was busy with the President's message; but the Congress would not convene until noon, and there was no knowing how long the routine opening formalities would take. Mr. Wilson, for whom the suspense of waiting had now become unbearable, eased his tension by indulging, despite the rain, in his favorite sport. He took to the golf course, while Congressional visitors to the White House were politely turned away.

In San Francisco's exclusive Bohemian Club, men were gravely discussing the probability of a German invasion from Mexico, first suggested by a story in the Los Angeles *Times*. The newspaper asserted that a huge German army was massing just south of the border, prepared to thrust north across the Rio Grande. Interest in the tong war racking Chinatown paled before this news.

The focus of popular thought and action lay in Washington, where already flags and bunting blossomed along Pennsylvania Avenue and the neighborhood of the Capitol. Special trains on the Pennsylvania and the Baltimore & Ohio railroads early began moving south from New York. An odd assortment of pilgrims was Washington-bound this

William D. (Big Bill) Haywood, head of the Industrial Workers of the World, the "Wobblies," was one of America's leading radicals. He stumped the nation preaching pacifism and begging America's workers to unite against the war.

Samuel Gompers, right, leader of the American Federation of Labor, seen here with President Wilson, supported the President's policies to the hilt. Shortly before America's declaration of war, Gompers summoned his union chieftains to Washington where they pledged organized labor's services to Wilson without reservation.

morning, both on the specials and on the regularly scheduled trains.

The President's *éminence grise,* "Colonel" (by grace of the governor of Texas) Edward M. House, whose peace-seeking peregrinations through European chancelleries at Wilson's behest had both flabbergasted and amused cynical diplomats, was coming down from his New York home; and a delegation of suffragettes of the Women's National Party, led by Mrs. Carrie Chapman Catt and all in high fettle, were on their way to escort to the Capitol Jeannette Rankin, first woman elected to Congress. The Sixteenth Amendment, granting universal suffrage to women, had still two lingering years to face before ratification, but some states had already recognized their women. So Miss Rankin's debut in the House of Representatives would be a shining milestone.

The major group of pilgrims, one which worried Washington police,

Thomas J. Z. Mooney, West Coast Socialist and pacifist,
was sentenced to death, along with Warren K. Billings,
for his alleged part in a bomb explosion that
disrupted a San Francisco preparedness parade in 1916.
Their sentences were later commuted to life imprisonment.

was bent on opposing the Presidential message. It had been organized
by the Emergency Peace Foundation, the brain child of William Jennings Bryan, the "Great Commoner" and three times a candidate for
President, and Detroit's Henry Ford, whose millions backed the Foundation. According to the anti-war New York *Call,* the Socialist Labor
Party organ and selfappointed press agent for the pacifist movement,
20,000 men and women from New York, Philadelphia and Baltimore
were on the way.

Despite the *Call's* boasts, organized labor did not seem to have much
to do with this invasion. Samuel Gompers, leader of the American
Federation of Labor, was no pacifist. He was at the moment more concerned with curbing radicals such as the "Wobblies," William D. ("Big
Bill") Haywood's Industrial Workers of the World.

West Coast Socialist firebrands Thomas J. Z. Mooney and Warren K. Billings might well have assumed leadership of the labor pacifist element, but they were unavoidably detained at San Quentin Prison, serving life sentences for their parts in the bomb explosion that marred the San Francisco Preparedness Parade of 1916.

Mrs. Henry Villard, president of the Women's Peace Party and widowed mother of Oswald Garrison Villard, pacifist editor of the New York *Evening Post,* was expected to lead the widely publicized march on Washington, but at the last minute the seventy-three-year-old Mrs. Villard reneged.

But another West Coast pacifist, of entirely different character, was available: Dr. David Starr Jordan, mild-mannered, sincere chancellor of Stanford University and director of the World Peace Foundation. And Jordan agreed to assume command despite the roughing-up he had

Chosen to lead a group of pacifists in a march on Washington as the President called upon Congress for a declaration of war, was Dr. David Starr Jordan, chancellor of Stanford University. Two days before the march he was roughed-up by "patriots."

Arch-enemy of preparedness, champion of peace,
Senator Robert Marion La Follette, of Wisconsin,
was the leader of the Progressive party.
As the pacifists marched on Washington,
the Senator tried desperately to get
authorization for them to hold a formal
demonstration in front of the Capitol. He failed.
Later, La Follette voted against America's entry into the war.

undergone less than forty-eight hours earlier in Baltimore's Academy of Music at the hands of a mob of rowdy "patriots", who stormed his pacifist mass meeting singing "We'll hang Dave Jordan to a sour apple tree!"

Also pounding the rails to Washington were members of the hurriedly organized "Pilgrims for Patriotism," rallied by the National Security League to offset the pacifist march. James Gordon Bennett's New York *Herald,* an active exponent of the League's principles and those of its leaders—former President Theodore Roosevelt, Major General Leonard Wood, Alton B. Parker, Joseph H. Choate, and other silk-stocking Republicans—asserted that 35,000 "Pilgrims" would leave New York on special trains departing "every five minutes."

Senator Henry Cabot Lodge, of Massachusetts,
long a leading and determined war hawk, was baited
in his senate office by a group of pacifists.
Called a "damned liar," the aging solon
lashed out and knocked down his young tormentor with one blow.

Accordingly, Washington reporters flocked to Union Station to cover the invasion, while police hastily announced that there would be no parades—either for or against war—this day in Washington. The "Pilgrims for Patriotism," evidently warned of the ban, failed to materialize as a body. But the pacifists, reduced in number to a few hundred, arrived to rally under Dr. Jordan.

Their ardor, already dampened by the rain, received another chill when the Washington police ban was announced. They milled around, footloose in the bunting-hung city, repulsed by watchful policemen in turn from the White House and the State, War and Navy Building, while Senator Robert Marion La Follette of Wisconsin, leader of the radical progressives, threw his weight around in a vain effort to obtain a parade permit. In their wanderings about the Capitol area, one small group—Massachusetts people all—sought and found real trouble.

Emotionally-torn, Congresswoman Jeanette Rankin voted against America's entry into the war and then slumped down in her seat in tears.

Jeanette Rankin, from a campaign photograph.

Invading Senator Henry Cabot Lodge's rooms in the Senate Office Building, they noisily demanded audience. When the Senator appeared, one Alexander Bannwart, thirty-six-year-old son of Swiss-German parents, angrily addressed him as "a damned coward," the while making threatening gestures. Lodge, sixty-seven years of age and a long-time exponent of positive action against the Central Powers, squared off nimbly and knocked Bannwart down, as Capitol police swarmed over the pacifist group. The bleeding Bannwart rode away in a paddy wagon, while Lodge became the hero of the moment.

At high noon both Senate and House convened to run through the formalities of opening a new session of Congress. In the House the occasion was marked by the appearance of the lady from Montana, Miss Jeannette Rankin. Hatless, wearing a green dress and carrying a bouquet of flowers, she received a standing ovation from the floor as she took her seat, while in the visitor's gallery Mrs. Catt's exuberant suffragettes, who had escorted their champion up the Capitol steps, loudly cheered.

Over in the Senate the routine opening procedure was promptly disposed of and an adjournment taken. But in the House the members

droned on for several hours. Meanwhile Mr. Wilson, back from his golf, had snatched a bite of lunch and read the text of his message to his family and Colonel House. The Colonel, it seemed, was delighted with the wording of the message; later he noted in his memoirs that none of the Wilson papers had pleased him more

Then the President went over to the State, War and Navy Building. Closeted for a while with Secretary of War Newton D. Baker, he moved next to the Navy Department, sat in with Secretary Josephus Daniels at a meeting of the Navy's General Board, then returned to the White House to receive word that the Congress would be ready to receive him at half past eight o'clock. The President and his family, together with Colonel House, sat down at seven to a hasty dinner.

Over at Fort Myer, across the Potomac, a squadron of the 2nd Cavalry was preparing to turn out as evening approached. Jittery folk in high places, it seemed, feared disorder, so one troop had been detailed to escort the President to and from the Capitol, while two others would reinforce the scores of police, Secret Service men, and even Post Office inspectors, who had been hurriedly gathered to ring the Capitol against hecklers and perhaps worse. Some of the blasé horse soldiers were making book, as soldiers will, on how long this particular soirée would last. They were not overly enthusiastic about it, for they had a slippery ten-mile round trip to make, sitting in wet saddles, and there was no knowing how long the President would speak. Tobacco-chewing consensus was that it would be midnight at best before they got back, finished grooming wet mounts, and stumbled into their warm barracks.

In Washington itself, people were gathering quietly along Pennsylvania Avenue and around the Capitol, despite the rain—warmer rain, now—that sprinkled the streets and soaked the bunting over the storefronts. No estimate is available of their number, but it must have been considerable. However, people in Washington were gathering also that evening for other purposes. The Columbia Theater, where George M. Cohan was making his motion-picture debut in *Broadway Jones,* was filling up, and so, too, were the Keith and the Belasco. But the great event of the day—the crucial event—was about to unfold in the Capitol. Its hero was on the way there now.

Josephus Daniels, Secretary of the Navy, and dean of President
Wilson's cabinet was, until the outbreak of the war, best
known as the man responsible for the banning of hard liquor
on the nation's dreadnaughts and at shore stations. His undersecretary
was a young, attractive New Yorker, Franklin Delano Roosevelt.

THE FIRST DAY/*Part Two*

"Make the World Safe for Democracy"

"All the News That's Fit to Print."

The New York Times.

THE WEATHER
Rain today; colder at night; Tuesday overcast; colder; south winds.
For full weather report see Page 21.

XVI...NO. 21,618.   NEW YORK, MONDAY, APRIL 2, 1917.—TWENTY-TWO PAGES.   ONE CENT In Greater New York. | TWO CENTS New England and Middle States. | THREE CENTS Elsewhere.

PRESIDENT'S WAR MESSAGE, READY FOR CONGRESS, WHICH MEETS TODAY; LITTLE STIR IN BERLIN OVER NEW FOE

EATS BACK HREE MILES ST. QUENTIN

ve Germans Out of est of City, After vy Fighting.

INDENBURG LINE

boring Frantically to Concrete Emplace- and Dugouts.

'IN WAS PILLAGED

In Ruins, While Mu- en Looted.

PHILIP CROSS.

THE NEW YORK TIMES 'RESPONDENT'S HEAD' 1, (Dispatch to The Chronicle.)—Eleven villes soil upon which their son gives back to France troops after a week-end the whole Department of now been cleared of Ger- nan ago that would have most miraculous achieve- by the German abandon- th trench positions under of great gunfire this ... is no longer astonishing. dvanced posts of cavalry ntry detachments holding- until the pressure of German strength is now ... during the, to which the ... vasn very close by the ... y at dawn today. Three ... four miles from St. ... the high grounds that ... of fury the spires of ... dral are visible, point- hollow in which the town wn in that hollow thirty ... spelling the beautiful ... edral St. ... ... rin St. Quentin was and ... Bonne for German ... the battle line until ... aws a series of explo- ... apart at least of St. ... in, like all the smaller ... hborhood. Its mason- and its picture galleries ... es of all their treasures. ... n of the Hindenburg is ... o swashed about with ... protected by barricades ... The Siegfried defences ... the German line of de- ... ng hard to complete it, ... emplacements, timber- ... trenches, and filling up ... vill exit here and there, ... terfering on account of ... They held the plain ... 600 Prussians of the ... iegfried Division. The ... roached before they at- ... although the British ... regular bombardment ... the place with regular- ... ncasualties were in ... ead Germans in shambles ... and fifty prisoners were ... udden dash forward or ... se rest got away with ...

now threatened by ... wn every close by the ... will make a breach to ... line, which now com- ... with fixed positions ... stood upon the Somme ...

TOP RIDGE E CATELET

y, Crest of High here the Germans to Stand.

1.—By the capture of ry, west of St. Quentin ..od, a mile northeast of ...ritish troops are within ... city. Between them ... s line a ridge which ... ...wartedly direction from ... Roghty to Gouseau- ... ...erni Hale's troops are ... crest of the ridge at ... to a height of 420 ... ...ved in some quarters ... ...will continue to push ... ...ightly toward Le Catel ... ...the Germans out of ... partharn farther ...

... with the British ... ...rmans with three fixed ... t quantity of war ma- ... ...the beginning of ... ...70 officers and 4,000 ...

British report reads as ... 9th of March we have ... ...nd local operations ... ...the of the enemy's with- ... ...man prisoners, includ- ... ..nd have captured 2 ... ...h mortars, and ...5 ... ...soners captured in the ...

...he kiddies laugh the ... ...h Fox, most whimsical ... ...and his antics clubbed ... ...he Evening Post and ... ...Catch The New York ...

HOLMES WON'T FIGHT SO OFFERS TO RESIGN

Trustees Call Pacifist Pastor an Impractical Idealist, but Won't Drop Him.

ASSAILS NATION IN SERMON

"No Order of a President Can Force Me to the Business of Killing," He Declares.

A plea that his congregation bear with his views and allow him to con- tinue his pastorate, though he was will- ing to surrender it upon demand, was made by Dr. John Haynes Holmes yes- terday in the course of a pacifist ser- mon, in which the clergyman asserted that under no circumstances would he give military service to the country.

It was Dr. Holmes who sponsored the Anti-enlistment League, urging young men to pledge themselves not to volun- teer for service in a foreign war, and who very recently caused the American flag to be taken down from in front of his church and draped over the com- munion table inside " because its public display might tend to inflame the public mind."

Dr. Holmes said in his sermon:

"When hostilities begin, it is uni- versally assumed that there is but a single service which a loyal citizen can render to the State, that of bearing arms and killing the enemy. Will you under- stand me if I say, humbly and regret- fully, that this I cannot and will not do. If any man or boy in this church ap- proaches the call to arms, I shall bless him as he marches to the front.

"No order of a President or a Gov- ernor will persuade me or force me to this business of killing. The issue be- fore me at least—there is no compro- mise—once me is here. The churches will be called upon to enlist, as will every other social institution. Therefore would I make it plain that so long as I can, my minister the Church of the Messiah will answer no military summons. Other clergymen may go to God for strength for one army; I will not In this church, if nowhere else in all America, the Ger- man will still be remembered as a broth- er; God's children. No word of hatred shall be spoken against them, no evil wish sent forth against their souls.

"I will commemorate without distinction the peoples of all lands who bear the dread burden of war this day, the issue for us all—to God for victory or death."

Dr. Holmes reaffirmed his declaration that war is hellish and inexcusable un- der any circumstances, [thundered against universal service and declared he would serve his country by working for the universal brotherhood after the war. He is an ardent disciple of Romaine Rolland, French author, who has been banished from his native land for propagating similar views.

Addison J. Andrews, a Trustee of the church, said:

"Dr. Holmes is an idealist. His ser- mon yesterday held up the ideal. But whether war is practical. This isn't the time to put his idealism into practice. We are not going to drop him, but the Ger- many or anybody else will wipe up the floor with us. We are going to fight first. The Church of the Messiah is going to fight first, and I think Dr. Holmes along with the rest of us. He makes a nice distinction, and in theory how impractical into distinctive, in the way he doesn't think there will be any demand for his resignation. I would not favor such demand. Let him hold his views. We need both sides. In part he is right. At any rate, he always is on other matters."

FIRST TROOPS LEAVE CITY ON SECRET ORDERS

71st Regiment and Battalion of the 23d Are Now in Active Service.

OFFICERS AND MEN PROUD

Colonel Bates Announces That Every Man in His Regiment Responded to Call.

WAIT IN BROOKLYN ARMORY

Soldiers Had Hoped to Get Away in Morning, but Could Not Leave Until 6:45 P. M.

Nearly 2,000 National Guardsmen of Manhattan and Brooklyn—the Seventy- first Regiment and a Battalion of the Twenty-third Regiment of Infan- try, respectively—left their armories un- der secret orders yesterday—the first State troops to be sent on active service since the issuance of the President's or- der for mobilization. The departure of the Seventy-first from its armory at Park Avenue and Thirty-third Street was preceded by a prayer by the Chaplain of the regiment, the Rev. William F. Crockett. Colonel William G. Bates made a brief address, in which he told his men he had the utmost confidence they would do their duty, no matter what that entailed or where they were sent. Both officers and men were proud of the fact that their organization was the first complete National Guard unit to be called out in this State for work in the new crisis.

Unaccompanied by a band and dressed in their field service uniforms with 16 many cases had been worn on long dusty hikes on the Mexican border, the members of the Seventy-first left the armory about 5 A. M., and with quick strides marched west to Thirty- fourth Street to Fifth Avenue. The sidewalks were lined with cheering friends and relatives. The men marched north on Fifth Avenue to Fortieth Street, Depot to Sixth Avenue, to Forty-second Street, and to the railroad station.

A little later the second and third detachments left the armory and marched to different railroad stations, each battalion having a different as- signment. About 1,300 men of the Sev- enty-first left the city for duty yester- day.

During the afternoon the field equipment was carried from the armory to the stations in trucks provid- ed by the Motor Truck Club of Ameri- ca. This equipment included cook stoves, extra clothes, rifles, and ammunition. There were 170,000 pounds of it, but the National Guardsmen assigned to the task of moving this mountain of sup- plies quickly went about it with a dex- terity and skill acquired during Mexican border service, which enabled them practically to complete the task by late afternoon.

Every man in the Seventy-first re- sponded to the call to arms—the second within a year—before the regiment left the city yesterday, according to Colonel Bates. Those who over the call when the call was issued hurried back, and when definite instructions to move out of the city were given they cheered at the prospect of active service and of getting out of the armory, to which they had been restricted daily. There were affecting farewell scenes both at the armory and at the railroad stations when the men were getting ready to leave. Relatives had gathered at both places, and the men were allowed to talk to them until the final hours blew.

The four companies of the Third Bat- talion of the Twenty-third Regiment, which has the armory at Bedford and Atlantic Avenues, in Brooklyn, were objects of envy among the members of the other two battalions of the regi- ment, who have been mobilized but have not received orders for active service. Their fellow-guardsmen gathered at the armory to "see them off." So did hundreds of friends and relatives. The farewells lasted nearly all day, for the men had hoped to get away during the morning, and it was 6:45 P. M. before they left. They marched to the subway station at Flatbush and Atlantic Ave- nues and thence to the Grand Central Station. Major John B. Sawyer, who was in charge of the battalion, declared it was in perfect condition and that the men were eager for action.

Unlike the Seventy-first, these men had been ordered to mobilize on Satur- day, and the mustering into the Federal service had to be rushed to be com- pleted in time for them to leave yes- terday. The other two battalions of the regiment have not yet been mustered in. The First Battalion will, however, be mustered in today. Reports were current among the rest of the men that tattoos were to be sent out for active today or tomorrow. The First ...

RIOT AT BALTIMORE ENDS PEACE MEETING

Great Crowd Invades Hall Where Jordan Is Speaking—Banker and Others Clubbed.

BALTIMORE, April 1.—After the greatest patriotic demonstration this city has seen since the Spanish-Ameri- can war, a crowd of 4,000 persons stormed the Academy of Music tonight, swept a cordon of police aside, and smashed a big pacifist meeting to bits, stopping Dr. David Starr Jordan in the middle of a word and refusing to allow the speaking to continue.

Police reserves from all over the city were called out and broke up the crowd with their clubs, beating several young men unmercifully and arresting two wagonloads of men. One man, Douglas G. Ober, gave as badly beaten that he was taken to a hospital. The meeting was handled by the pacifist work- ers of the American Union Against Mili- tarism, whose President is David Starr Jordan, and Louis Merryman ... about ...

Dr. Jordan was beginning his plea for peace the crowd of anti-pacifists, composed of business men, profess- ors of schools and colleges in the city, and students from the same, made a rally through a cordon of police and rushed down the aisles of the theatre where they demanded that their ...

In the front ranks were President Robert W. Wood of Johns Hopkins Uni- versity, Professor John H. Latané of Johns Hopkins, Douglas Ober, Gustavus Ober, Jr., D. H. Mason Knox, Jacob H. France, Bartlett E. Johnson, E. Lancaster Williams of Middendorf, Williams & Co., Major Adams, J. R. Crawford Frost, and other business men and members of the Faculties of Johns Hopkins, University of Maryland, City College, Baltimore Polytechnic Institute, and Mount St. Joseph's College.

The peace meeting was held under the auspices of the American League Against Militarism. The counter-dem- onstration was organized on the summons of the Academy of Music. Finally the crowd took into its own hands and led by some millionaire, broke into the theatre and marched down the aisles waving the American flag ...

Just as Dr. Jordan stepped onto the platform which broke into the theatre Carter G. Osborne, Jr., a banker, was at the head of the noisy crowd, clubbed him until he was unconscious. The crowd, seeing the flag disappear from his hand, leaped forward, swept the police aside, and got into the theatre.

PACIFIST CRUSADERS FAIL TO FILL TRAINS

Reserve Forty Cars and Muster Only Enough Opponents of Defense for Twelve.

PATRIOTS ARE RALLYING

Sure They Will Outnumber Pacifists Five to One in Washington— Prominent Men Join.

A special train that carried 300 mem- bers of the Emergency Peace Federa- tion from the Pennsylvania Station at 12:30 o'clock this morning for Washington, where the opponents of war plan to appeal directly to Congress to keep the country out of war. A simi- lar delegation went an hour later over the Baltimore & Ohio road from Jersey City.

Colonel Edward M. House, the Presi- dent's friend and adviser, went to Washington this morning, starting from the Pennsylvania Station about two minutes ahead of the peace delegation. The Colonel had a berth in the first sec- tion of the regular express, which de- parted at 12:30. The "peace special" followed the second section of the ex- press. When Colonel House passed through the station he saw about him groups of men and women of the peace party wearing white strips of cloth on coat sleeves bearing in large letters the cry: "Keep out of war."

Forty cars to run in four trains had been reserved for the pacifists, but when it came time to go it was found that all could be accommodated on one train of twelve sleepers and twenty-five berths each. It was expected by the leaders of the crusade that at least 3,000 would go by each road, and the fact that no more than one-third as many appeared was a keen disappoint- ment.

There were about fifty women in the pilgrimage. While the women were waiting for the train to be made up, a representative of the committee distrib- uted "The Hague Peace Flower," giv- ing each of the women a white button, showing the leaders were Miss Emily Green Balch, Professor of Economics at Wellesley College, and Dr. David Starr Jordan.

Each person paid his own expenses. It was said, and the $45,000 that was collected by the federation for the peace campaign will be spent for meet- ing halls, headquarters, &c., except for the sum that has already been expended for newspaper advertising.

The New York pacifists will join dele- gations from other cities in Washing- ton. They will hold meetings, pass out peace circulars, and engage in such demonstrations as are not taboo under the terms of the Washington police. A police order stopped the proposed peace pa- rade, but the leaders say that they will make some kind of "dignified demon- stration" either before the President or Congress, or perhaps both.

Thousands of persons from this city representing nearly every walk of life, will join the patriotic pilgrimage to Washington today to represent those who want war declared against Germany at once. Leaders in the movement said last night at the Hotel Belmont, where headquarters were opened, that their three days' work had resulted in an overwhelming response and that their opponents, the pacifists, who left for the capital early this morning, would be out- numbered five to one.

Although they will start a few hours behind that group which is demanding peace with Germany, notwithstanding the U-boat warfare, the patriot legions say they will arrive in ample time and feel no alarm over the pacifist invasion. Among those who have personally notified the committee arranging the patriotic demonstration that they expect to be in Washington on Monday are Judge E. H. Lacombe, Frank C. Vanderlip, Thomas W. Lamont, John P. Agar, George B. Agnew, Irving T. Bush, W. S. Kies, Richard S. Childs, and Professor Charles S. Baldwin. There has been no attempt to enlist pilgrims by organizations. Every one will go as an individual.

Officials have for weeks made a study of the attitude of the United States toward the Vienna Government. When relations were broken off Germany they were not served with their passports as an ally. Austria-Hungary. The Washington officials made inquiries and Ambassador Penfield reported that Aus- tria's attitude toward American ships and toward other peaceful merchant ships which neither resisted nor fled was humanitarian. The Austro-Gov- ernment made a reply which was phrased in a certain conciliatory spirit was far from satisfactory to this Gov- ernment.

Friends of Reform Encouraged.

The passage by the Reichstag on Friday of a resolution for the creation of a commission to discuss constitutional reforms is generally considered a signal triumph for the forces of progress. The overwhelming vote in its favor indicated that to the reform element in the coun- try has gained much ground lately.

APPRECIATES OUR STRENGTH

But Prefers War With America to Modifying U-Boat Activities.

PRAISE FOR AMERICAN NAVY

Persius Warns Germans Against Accepting Criticisms of It Made at Home.

EXPECT INTERNAL REFORMS

Observers See Fair Prospects for an Early Liberalization of Imperial Government.

New Disturbances in Berlin Reported by Way of Holland

Special Cable to THE NEW YORK TIMES.
BERLIN, April 1 (via London.)— Never in the history of nations, per- haps, has there been so little excite- ment on the eve of war between two great countries as at present in Ger- many. Everybody knows that within a few days America will declare war against Germany, but no one seems par- ticularly impressed by it. The attach- ment for reform naturally absorbs all interest here, while the revolution in Russia assumes second place in the minds of the people, and war with America is hardly ever discussed. It is accepted as an unavoidable vicissi- tude of fate that must be borne in the best way possible.

At the same time it must not be sup- posed that America's military and na- val power are underestimated. On the contrary, every responsible persons, or even the people at large, minimize the weight of moral and financial aid that America can bring to the support of Germany's ene- mies. But since the alternative is to give up the U-boat war or face an American war, the people will prefer the latter, for nothing can change their conviction that the submarines will end the war.

Little News from America.

The news from America is exceedingly scant, the papers publishing seldom more than 200 or 300 words daily, mostly extracts from French papers, the cor- respondents of which seem absolutely ig- norant of things and wars American. Their reports on America's war prep- arations base the stamp of fantastic ex- aggeration, and one cannot help sus- pecting that Reuter has surrendered to them the monopoly of supplying Ger- many with American "war news" for obvious purposes.

None of the papers has commented officially on the American situation within the last few days, their columns being filled with sensational speeches for or against reform delivered in the Prussian Lower House and Reichstag, which were in sessions here until last evening.

Persius Appreciates Our Navy Slightly.

The evening Tageblatt prints an article by Captain Persius on "The North American Navy." He protests against the idea, which he says is widely prevalent, that the American Navy need not be feared much, although it is at least as large as the German Navy since, although composed of very large ships, it suffers from a deficiency of crews. With all due respect to Captain Persius, I feel bound to say that com- petent critics here, at least, have a very small opinion of the American Navy. They are too well informed to permit themselves to be deceived by at- tacks on its efficiency like that of George von Langelee Meyer in The Yale Review, which they attribute to confid- erations of party politics.

Captain Persius, in his article, em- phasizes the good qualities of the Ameri- can Navy, especially its strength in battleships and its effective distribution of artillery. He says the crews prove true to their splendid traditions in case of emergency and Baldwin states, which, however, took place recently next to the country to guard against. When relations were broken off Germany they were not served with their passports as an ally. Austria-Hungary. The Washington officials made inquiries and Ambassador Penfield reported that Aus- tria's attitude toward American ships and toward other peaceful merchant ships which neither resisted nor fled was humanitarian. The Austro-Gov- ernment made a reply which was phrased in a certain conciliatory spirit was far from satisfactory to this Gov- ernment.

Washington to Keep a Tight Rein on Pacifists; No Chance to Parade, Demonstrate, or Pacify

Special to The New York Times.
WASHINGTON, April 1.—When the hordes and counter-hordes of pacifists and patriots come piling into town tomorrow they will make, not a demonstration but a whirlpool. They can't parade, they can't "demon- strate," they can just be in Washington. The authorities have set their faces against any parading or demonstrating. They may go to the Capitol and buttonhole Congressmen, but that has to be done in accord- ance with the Capitol rules; no impromptu mass meetings are to be held in the corridors. When the President makes his address, admission to the galleries and the building will be by ticket, and nobody will be admitted who cannot satisfy the authorities that he does not intend to start any row or demonstration.

How many of the invaders will be here no one can estimate. The pa- cifists, who began first, did not have time to complete this thing scien- tifically, and the other side has had still less time. They will be coming in by trainloads all day tomorrow, but neither side knows how many are coming or what will be done with them when they get here. The pacifists have the advantage of having started earlier, and have arranged a pro- gram of meetings, but they do not know what they are going to do at the meetings. They have captured Convention Hall, with a business meeting tomorrow morning, another in the afternoon, and a mass meeting in the evening, with another business meeting on Tuesday morning, but that serves no real purpose except to keep the patriots out, for the pro- gram is so indefinite that nobody knows even who is to preside at the meetings.

The pacifists have sent communications to a number of labor organ- izations, asking for delegates, but to do it informally, without waiting for the usual convening of councils and other authoritative bodies. The "delegates" will therefore be individuals instead of delegations. It is evident from the way they talk that they are leaning rather heavily on the support they expect to get from labor, but they do not seem to know how far that dependence is justified.

The city will be treated to this spectacle from morning till night. When they arrive here there is nothing much they can do except to move on the Capitol, and, as already explained, they will have to do that under regulations. But the purpose of the pacifist drive, since the parading was called off by the police, is to impress Congress by their numbers, and to that end an incessant pilgrimage will be conducted from the moment the members reach the Capitol. It is to be assumed that the patriots will adopt the same tactics and that the lobbies will be full of contending but- tonholers.

NO BREAK WITH US, AUSTRIA SAYS

Ambassador Penfield Expected to Return to Vienna in Three Months.

ATTACHES STAY AT POSTS

Lansing Will Neither Admit Nor Deny That Envoy Has Been Called Home.

AMSTERDAM, April 1.—Telegraphing from Vienna, the correspondent of the semi-official Norddeutsche Allgemeine Zeitung of Berlin says:

"With a view to obtaining all infor- mation here, we are authorized to state that the journey of Frederic C. Pen- field, the American Ambassador, to Washington means no change in the re- lations between Austria-Hungary and the United States.

"Diplomatic intercourse continues to be maintained, and is looked after by our Chargé d'Affaires in Washington and by the American Chargé d'Affaires here. Mr. Penfield is expected to re- turn to Vienna in three months."

Special to The New York Times.
WASHINGTON, April 1.—Secretary Lansing tonight declined to deny or af- firm the statement cabled unofficially from London to the effect that Frederic Courtland Penfield, the American Am- bassador to Austria-Hungary, had been called home for a conference. Mr. Lansing said he was unwilling at this time to make any comment on the rela- tions between this country and Austria- Hungary, and had received no notifica- tion that Mr. Penfield had left Vienna.

According to the News Press Service of Vienna, as reported by Reuter's Amsterdam correspondent, Ambassador Penfield and Mrs. Penfield were about to depart for Washington at the re- quest of the State Department, which "urgently desires his presence and ad- vice regarding matters connected with the war." The failure of the American State to deny this news report that Mr. Penfield had been called home had the inevitable effect of inspiring the belief that there was some substantial foun- dation for the Vienna report that Mr. Penfield was coming home for a con- ference.

Officials have for weeks made a study of the attitude of the United States toward the Vienna Government. When relations were broken off Germany they were not served with their passports as an ally. Austria-Hungary. The Washington officials made inquiries and Ambassador Penfield reported that Aus- tria's attitude toward American ships and toward other peaceful merchant ships which neither resisted nor fled was humanitarian. The Austro-Gov- ernment made a reply which was phrased in a certain conciliatory spirit was far from satisfactory to this Gov- ernment.

Friends of Reform Encouraged.

The passage by the Reichstag on Friday of a resolution for the creation of a commission to discuss constitutional reforms is generally considered a signal triumph for the forces of progress. The overwhelming vote in its favor indicated that to the reform element in the coun- try has gained much ground lately.

GARDNER TO OFFER WAR DECLARATION

Massachusetts Member Wants Action Taken by Congress to be Unequivocal.

FAVORS OUTRIGHT ALLIANCE

Sees Our Own Ultimate Safety at Stake—Would Send Ad- vance Guard to Trenches.

Special to The New York Times.
WASHINGTON, April 1.—Repre- sentative Gardner of Massachusetts, who has been active in the fight for American preparedness, today announced that he would offer a resolution tomorrow de- claring war on Germany in unequivocal terms. Mr. Gardner said he didn't know the fine distinction between declaring war and declaring that a state of war existed, but the declaration of a state of war seemed to him an admission that the United States had been kicked about a good deal, and he wanted the declaration of Congress to make it plain that the United States was going to kick back.

Mr. Gardner said that he favored the sending of a army and a force to show his American sympathy with the Allies and the sending of as many de- stroyers as possible to hunt down German submarines. As fast as pos- sible, he wanted a strong army fitted out and trained for actual participation in the war, and, to prevent the Allies from making peace while the United States was still at war with Germany, he wanted the United States to enter into a pledge with the Allies against a separate peace by any of the enemies of Germany.

Mr. Gardner's statement follows:

"Whatever history may say about Woodrow Wilson, I am confident that, in the matter of holding Germany to ac- countability, he will be acquitted of the charge of having acted with unseemly haste. At least it begins to look as if the American eagle is really on the war- path. I hope that it has flown so far already that it cannot retire to the dovecote again for another dream.

"However, in the last two years I have seen so many crises float harm- lessly downstream that I am not quite easy when Congress has actually de- clared war. Many folks say that it means merely the same thing if Congress declares that a state of war exists. I am not an international lawyer, and I don't quite understand the hair-splitting distinction, but I hope that we shall make a declaration which admits of only one interpretation.

"This business of declaring that Ger- many has been making war on us seems to me like announcing that Germany has been murdering us all over the lot. Of course, Germany has been killing us all over the lot; every man, woman, and child from China to Peru is as in- dignant as we are. The time has come to say to the whole world: 'The German Empire and its allies are the enemies of the United States.'

"The expectation exists that the President will not seek to tell Congress how many troops should be provided for to make the credit good to the purpose. I believe the matter of voting addi- tional revenue and making appropria- tions to make preparations for war, if ...

MAY SPEAK ON TUESDAY

President's Plans Depend on Time It Takes House to Organize.

FLAG-DECKED CITY IS CALM

Troops on Duty at All Strategic Points—Admission to Capi- tol to be by Card.

ORDERS READY FOR FLEET

Sentiment for Universal Train- ing Grows, but Call for Volunteers Likely.

Special to The New York Times.
WASHINGTON, April 1.—On this, the eve of the meeting of what may be the most momentous war Congress in the nation's history, Washington presents an unusual spectacle such as might be expected at a time when the country is about to engage in hostilities with a foreign power. The situation from the outward Washington standpoint does not afford a thrill.

President Wilson declared today he will deliver be- fore the two houses of Congress in which he will point the way for a dec- laration of war or a declaration that war exists between the United States and Germany. When he will deliver it has not been determined. The date of his appearance before Congress will depend on how long the House of Representa- tives, with its complex political compo- sition, takes to organize. As soon as or- ganization is completed the President will make his appearance, according to the understanding tonight. It is gen- erally accepted here that he will go to the Capitol on Tuesday afternoon, but the situation in the House makes it im- possible to hazard any accurate predic- tion.

Secretary Baker was at his desk in the War Department today, and there was evidence of unusual activity in the mili- tary bureaus of the department. Major Gen. Bliss, the Assistant Chief of the Army (General Staff, and other impor- tant officials were in consultation with the Secretary. In the Navy Depart- ment Secretary Daniels was on duty, actively giving orders and conferring with his chief subordinates. It was evi- dent that the navy was sending out or- ders to warships and navy yards, and that when the word was given that war would be ready to carry out the naval instructions given to their commanders.

In hot lobbies groups of Congress- men make it apparent that a session of Congress is about to begin. Mem- bers there is an insistent discussion among them. The old-timers who are recogniz- ing here for new terms are convinced that President Wilson's address will be a preliminary to war, but it is generally admitted that inside information as to the President's position is lacking and nobody with the exception of Cabinet officers and a few others is able to speak by the card.

Sentiment for Universal Service.

The most striking and significant thing in the comment of the newly arrived Senators and Representatives is the seeming heavy sentiment in favor of universal military service. This wide- spread feeling affords ground for the belief that if the President comes out with a real recommendation for the conscription policy Congress will respond af- firmatively and the patriot element will prevail, and the House and the Senate will approve his recommendation. In the most promising quarters the ratio of opin- ion seems, however, that in his ad- dress to the Senate and the House the President will not make any recom- mendation with regard to means of rais- ing an army to help in the defeat of any enemy, but will simply ask for gen- eral authority to employ the land and naval forces of the United States against the powers of the German Empire and to call for volunteers.

THE FIRST DAY/Part Two

"Make the World Safe for Democracy"

IT WAS AFTER EIGHT O'CLOCK that night when the Presidential limousine wheeled out of the White House driveway to be swallowed up by its escort of bobbing cavalry and swept down Pennsylvania Avenue—a clattering mass of horses and poncho-draped men all shiny in the rain. Street lights reflected sparks from drawn sabers, emphasized the nervousness of horses skittery on wet pavement. In the shadows, flags and bunting hung limp and soggy.

Behind the cortege rolled a following wave of applause from the bystanders along the avenue—a wave that rose to a roar at last as the big motorcar burst from its living cocoon of horseflesh at the east portico of the Capitol. There a considerable crowd had gathered, kept at safe distance by the remainder of the cavalry and the police. The President disappeared inside, to a final burst of applause.

In the blazing lights of the House Chamber waited the members of the House and their guests—the Senate, the Supreme Court, the Cabinet. Also present—for what was said to be the first time on such occasion in the nation's history—was the entire diplomatic corps, all in panoply of full dress (minus, of course, the German delegation, who had received their *congé* a month ago).

Above the gathering, the press gallery bulged with correspondents, who remarked particularly that, with the exception of Senators La Follette and James K. Vardaman of Mississippi and perhaps a few others, each Senator carried or wore in his breast pocket a small American flag.

In the front row of the equally crowded visitors' gallery the chosen guests included Mrs. Wilson, the President's daughter Margaret, his cousin, Miss Helen Woodrow Bones, Colonel House, and Joseph P. Tumulty, the President's confidential secretary, all of whom had accompanied him from the White House.

The clock hands pointed to 8:35 as Champ Clark of Missouri, veteran Speaker of the House just reelected at the morning session, rose and banged his gavel.

*In a calm, cold voice, little betraying the seething emotion
pent-up inside him, President Woodrow Wilson,
the evening of April 2, 1917, before a joint session
of the Sixty-fifth Congress, called for war with Germany.
As he finished, the Congress and their distinguished
guests rose as one, cheered at the
top of their lungs and waved small American flags.*

"The President of the United States!"

And through the open door emerged the almost sepulchral figure of the stern-faced, self-willed Woodrow Wilson, to meet the blast of a vociferous, cheering welcome such as no President had ever before received from a Congress. For two long minutes the ovation lasted, while the President moved to the rostrum, slowly laid his message before him, and gravely bowed.

The morning's New York *Tribune* had carried a provocative piece under the by-line of one C. W. Gilbert, questioning Mr. Wilson's ability to fire his audience. "Making war," pontificated Gilbert, "is a great act of the emotions and the will. Mr. Wilson is an intellectual. Can he make the country feel it should fight?"

Neither Mr. Gilbert nor the horse soldiers outside the building had cause for worry. The President took but thirty-six minutes to lay his case before a frenetically receptive audience. He spoke with his usual calm, but observers noted the trembling of his hands as he turned the pages before him.

His words carried his hearers with him, for they voiced the cold wrath of a frustrated man, distilled from the troubled soul of one who detested war. And his audience lapped it up, Chief Justice Edward D. White, his white felt hat waving high, leading each successive bedlam of applause.

"The German submarine warfare against commerce is a warfare against mankind....We will not choose the path of submission and suffer the sacred rights of our people to be ignored or violated....I advise that the Congress formally accept the status of belligerent... thrust upon it and exert all its power and employ all its resources to bring the Government of the German Empire to terms and end the war."

Mr. Wilson missed no bets in summarizing the overt German encroachments on America's soil and on American rights. Then he detailed his program for the future: Extension of large financial credits to the Allies; mobilization and utilization of all industrial resources; immediate equipment of the Navy, with particular stress on anti-submarine activities; procurement of a 500,000 man Army through universal service, with such additional calls for troops as might be necessary; and finally, a Congressional carte blanche to the executive, financed by taxation rather than by borrowing.

The President's message ended on a high note: "The world must be made safe for democracy....To such a task we can dedicate our lives

"Let Germany Do It"

By C. W. Gilbert

WASHINGTON, April 1.—We shall know in a day or perhaps two days whether it is the fault of democracy or the fault of President Wilson. Down here at the capital you are assured at every turn that it is the fault of democracy. "Democracies are never ready," is the universal formula; you might almost suppose it to be a reason for self-complacency, so cheerfully is it repeated. And by implication it is suggested that the President has only been waiting for the great, blundering, slow-thinking host of men at whose head he is placed to make up their minds. The great, blundering, slow-thinking host are making up their minds. Now is the President's chance. Is he himself ready? The speech to Congress will show.

Will a leader be disclosed, or a scholar incapable of escaping from the twilight zone of intellectual debate? Will Mr. Wilson tell the country what it is going to war for in such a way that a great burst of righteous feeling will go through the hearts of men, or will he file a legal brief against Germany?

Making war is a great act of the emotions and of the will. Mr. Wilson is an intellectual. Can he make the country feel that it should fight? These are the questions people are asking here who realize that the zeal with which the nation enters into the war will depend upon how successfully Mr. Wilson presents the issue and brings it within the range of common understanding and popular emotion.

There is a pathetic feeling here that somehow some act of Germany must be relied upon to bring the question down from the plane of intellectual cognition to the level where it can be felt and where it will stir the popular heart. "Let Germany do it" has been the policy right along. And it is still. You hear that after we have declared the existence of a state of war Germany may be counted upon to make us mean war with all our hearts and all our minds.

Mr. Wilson shrinks from war with almost physical revulsion. His ideals are the ideals of peace. It will be difficult for him to present this issue to the nation as anything more than a conflict which we enter because we couldn't avoid entering it. There is nothing inspiring in the thought of merely being sucked into the European maelstrom.

Yet it is plain that this is the mental picture Congress has. Congress is the most local minded body in the world. It is dazed by the realization that the Atlantic Ocean is not so broad as it supposed the Atlantic Ocean was. Congress does not think now. It merely acts on suggestion, the suggestion taking the form of all the press agent matter that has gone forth recently on declaring a state of war. If you ask Congress a question it replies "state of war" quite mechanically.

(Left) *A questioning article by C. W. Gilbert that appeared in the New York* Tribune *the morning President Wilson was to address the Congress and ask for war. In the thirty-six minutes it took the President to deliver his address, he more than allayed Gilbert's fears and fired the nation and its will to fight.*

(Right) *One of the pacifist voices that was missing when the Sixty-fifth Congress convened in 1917 was that of Charles Augustus Lindbergh, Sr., of Minnesota. After a bitter campaign, in which he was aided by his young son, Lindbergh was soundly defeated in the district he had represented since 1907.*

and our fortunes...the day has come when America is privileged to spend her blood...for the principles that gave her birth and happiness and the peace she has treasured. God helping her, she can do no other."

With few exceptions, Mr. Wilson's audience went wild as he concluded. Men were standing on their chairs, were pounding desks, as they cheered at the top of their lungs and waved the flags they carried. The Chief Justice was in tears; Secretary of Commerce William C. Redfield and France's Ambassador Jean Jules Jusserand were locked in one another's arms.

The principal exception was Senator La Follette, arch-enemy of preparedness, champion of pacifism on any terms, leader of what Wilson had called the "little group of willful men" who in the preceding Senate had filibustered to death the President's plan to arm American merchantmen. Smiling sardonically, his jaws chomping gum, La Follette now stood silently aloof, with arms folded, conspicuous in the

APRIL 2, 1917.

maelstrom. There was one other individual who might be mentioned, though no one at the time, apparently, gave thought to his absence. The little man who wasn't there was a dour Swede from Minnesota, who had been a Representative since 1907. He was absent this evening because his district last November had repudiated his loudly voiced pro-German pacifist tendencies, after a bitter campaign in which his young son had helped him. The man's name was Charles Augustus Lindbergh, Sr.

With dramatic suddenness Mr. Wilson strode through the plaudits of the Chamber and drove home through streets still crowded with cheering admirers. Reporters rushed to file the story, and ticking telegraph keys spread the news over the wires. Presses began rolling around the nation, turning out the extras that would be hawked through the streets by shrill-voiced newsboys. The word caught the East before the theaters emptied; the West, as people sat down to the evening meal. It was three o'clock in the morning on April 3 in London and Paris—just in time for the morning papers to gloat—while in Berlin the bad news began trickling in at four.

In Washington the *Post* extra was read and cheered in all the theaters. In New York the reception varied. In front of the *Herald's* baroque building on Herald Square, where crowds seethed and milled on election nights, comparatively few spectators had gathered. They read lackadaisically the great hand-lettered bulletin announcing war. Farther up Broadway at Forty-second Street—some people were still calling the intersection Longacre Square—in the Knickerbocker Hotel, Enrico Caruso's headquarters when in New York, there was not much stir at the elaborate bar under the famous Old King Cole mural. But in the twenty-odd theaters, from the New Amsterdam Roof where Will Rogers was starring, to the Hippodrome with its revolving stage, fountains and herd of elephants, and all the way down to Minsky's on the Bowery, audiences cheered and orchestras blared the "Star-Spangled Banner" when announcements were read from the stage. At the Empire, where *A Kiss for Cinderella* was showing, the scene was most emotional; people climbed onto their seats to roar their enthusiasm.

It remained for the sedate Metropolitan Opera House to put on a real show. The curtain had fallen on the second act of De Koven's *Canterbury Pilgrims,* with Margarette Ober, a German soprano, in the role of the Wife of Bath. In William K. Vanderbilt's box, Mrs. Oliver

Newspaper reaction to the President's address was strongly favorable. The nation was aroused and ready—almost eager, as this New York Herald *cartoon suggests—to cast aside her neutralist mantle and assume the posture of war.*

While Caruso and Galli-Curci
were the toast of the Met,
Mary Garden remained the darling of
opera clubbers and standees alike.

Harriman waved a copy of the *Evening Telegram* in the air. James W. ("Jimmie") Gerard, just returned from his post as ambassador to Germany, who, with his wife and the Lewis Iselins, was in another box, buttonholed a director of the Met and demanded that the news be read and the orchestra play the national anthem. The director—some accounts say it was Giulio Gatti-Casazza himself—unwisely rejoined that the opera company was neutral. At that, the irate Gerard leaned forward from his box and bellowed to the rustling, whispering audience:

"Three cheers for President Wilson!"

Propriety forgotten, the stiff-shirted, diamond-studded occupants of the Golden Horseshoe...New York's society...exploded in the pan-

*Laurette Taylor
was the heroine
as Annie in
"Out There" at the Globe.*

*Starring as Widowed Europe,
Ethel Barrymore
appeared in "Battle Cry."*

While President Wilson prepared to go before Congress to call for a declaration of war against Germany, pacifist leaders across the country stepped up their call for peace and non-involvement.

demonium of a high-school football rally; the orchestra broke into the "Star-Spangled Banner" and the entire opera house rocked. When the noise died down the curtain rose on the final act, and the Teutonic Miss Ober toppled in a dead faint, fitting sequel to a scene such as the Met had never seen before nor would again. But at Carnegie Hall, not many blocks away, where a pacifist meeting was in full cry, the news was received with hisses and catcalls.

While the rest of an anxious world was being electrified by the news, the principals and cast of the big event on Capitol Hill had drifted away. The House had lingered only long enough to dispose of war appropriations bills before adjourning. Then its Foreign Affairs Committee,

Enroute home, American Ambassador to Germany James W. Gerard is bid goodbye by Comte Andre d'Ormesson representing the French government.

under Representative Henry D. Flood of Virginia, drafted a joint resolution to declare war and went home. The rest of the audience had long since faded away; the Senate's Foreign Relations Committee would meet early next day to draft its war announcement.

In the White House, Woodrow Wilson and his family sat for some time in the Oval Room before retiring. The President, all present agreed, appeared relieved of the tension previously gripping him. All we know of Wilson's thoughts and reactions on this occasion are embraced in a twenty-five word remark made to Joe Tumulty on the return to the White House:

"Think what it was they were applauding. My message today was a message of death to our young men. How strange that they should applaud."

On that note, we watch the lights in the White House dim at the close of the second day of April, 1917.

It had been quite a day.

After returning from Capitol Hill that evening of April 2, President Wilson met with his wife and daughter and Colonel House in the Oval Room of the White House. Later that night he went to the Cabinet room with his private secretary, Joseph P. Tumulty. There the two men discussed the day's events. According to Tumulty, they talked for a while. Then the President broke down and wept, his head on the Cabinet table.

THE SECOND DAY

Uncertain Trumpets

WEATHER
d warmer to-day. To-morrow overcast and warmer, with obable rain. Strong northwest winds.
Full Report on Page 13

New York Tribune

First to Last — the Truth: News - Editorials - Advertisements

CIRCULATION
Over 100,000 Daily
Net Paid, Non-Returnable

XXVI No. 25,706 (Copyright 1917— The Tribune Ass'n.) TUESDAY, APRIL 3, 1917 * * * ONE CENT In New York City

, First ed U. S. , Is Sunk

l at Night Near Americans Be- To Be Lost

an Crew orted Rescued

able to Give Bat- Least Eleven n Missing

l 2.—The American has been sunk by a r an island off Brest. rew were rescued and ought into Brest. A men are missing, and held that they can be teamer was torpedoed a heavy sea was run-

atrol picked up nine- of the Aztec. Twen- re reported missing. ves Sharp, the Amer- or, was informed this the French govern- rpedoing of the Aztec ly cabled the State Washington. ..t of the American l proceed to Brest to tions of survivors of

val Crew 1 Men Missing, hington Learns

April 2.—French Ad- ches to the French to-night announcing hout warning of the erican merchantman, Aztec, by a German apparently Lieuten- esham and twelve ackets, constituting d of the vessel, had , that eleven of the ted missing. report said the Aztec, York to Havre, was ut warning yesterday The torpedo struck ps, emitting a power- ng the wireless out of

th the captain and bers of the crew, in to put off, apparently by the French patrol r three hours. The men are thought to d when the first boat mashed. containing the sec- eighteen men, is not d for, but the fact ... reported missing ef that it must have

Armed Ship nder U. S. Flag

teamship Aztec, sunk marine off an island he first armed Ameri- sel to sail from a port Atlantic. The cable American Consul at ght the news of the her owners, the Ori- Company, gave no ink- of her crew. er command of Cap- en, was manned by a e. Seventeen of this g the captain, were erican citizens:

, mate, 538 Fiftieth
ond mate, 85 Garfield n, Mass.
ird mate, 60 Burgess J.
ngineer, 218 Forbell
engineer, 85 Garfield n, Mass.
, engineer, 510 East nington, Del.
n, engineer, 839 Fif- Brooklyn.
steward, 111 Sacra- Francisco.
messman, New York ory).
radio operator, New directory).
327 Twenty-ninth no such address).
acomber, Honolulu; o, Honolulu; Ekila Fato Davis, Hawaii; i.

-Inch Guns

the Aztec fought a her undersea ad- been disclosed. Her wever, that she had since she was sunk night when a heavy he vessel was armed ns, one forward and y naval gunners. w moving freighter nage, steamed from e on March 18 with dstuffs and general more than $500,000. avre to-morrow and than 100 miles from pedoed. uilt in 1894 by the ding Company at England, for the ship Company. She January last by the Company, with of- y Place. She was long, 43 feet beam eck to keelson.

en on the Aztec y their relatives

The President Calls for War Without Hate

Washington, April 2.—At 8:30 o'clock this evening President Wilson, addressing both branches of the 65th Congress, assembled in the House of Representatives, called for war against an irresponsible and inhuman Imperial German Government, without rancor, selfish objects or enmity toward the German people, all to the end of making "the world itself at last free." The speech was received with tremendous enthusiasm. It follows in full:

I HAVE called the Congress into extraordinary session because there are serious, very serious, choices of policy to be made, and made immediately, which it was neither right nor constitutionally permissible that I should assume the responsibility of making.

On the 3d of February last I officially laid before you the extraordinary announcement of the Imperial German Government, that on and after the 1st day of February it was its purpose to put aside all restraints of law or of humanity and use its submarines to sink every vessel that sought to approach either the ports of Great Britain and Ireland or the western coasts of Europe, or any of the ports controlled by the enemies of Germany within the Mediterranean.

That had seemed to be the object of the German submarine warfare earlier in the war, but since April of last year the imperial government had somewhat restrained the commanders of its under-sea craft, in conformity with its promise then given to us that passenger boats should not be sunk, and that due warning would be given to all other vessels which its submarines might seek to destroy, when no resistance was offered or escape attempted, and care taken that their crews were given at least a fair chance to save their lives in their open boats. The precautions taken were meagre and haphazard enough, as was proved in distressing instance after instance in the progress of the cruel and unmanly business, but a certain degree of restraint was observed.

Final Indictment Of German Frightfulness

The new policy has swept every restriction aside. Vessels of every kind, whatever their flag, their character, their cargo, their destination, their errand, have been ruthlessly sent to the bottom without warning and without thought of help or mercy for those on board, the vessels of friendly neutrals along with those of belligerents. Even hospital ships and ships carrying relief to the sorely bereaved and stricken people of Belgium, though the latter were provided with safe conduct through the prescribed areas by the German government itself, and were distinguished by unmistakable marks of identity, have been sunk with the same reckless lack of compassion or of principle.

I was for a little while unable to believe that such things would in fact be done by any government that had hitherto subscribed to the humane practices of civilized nations. International law had its origin in the attempt to set up some law, which would be respected and observed upon the seas, where no nation had right of dominion and where lay the free highways of the world. By painful stage after stage has that law been built up, with meagre enough results, indeed, after all was accomplished that could be accomplished, but always with a clear view at least of what the heart and conscience of mankind demanded.

Because It Had No Weapons But These

This minimum of right the German government has swept aside under the plea of retaliation and necessity, and because it had no weapons which it could use at sea except these, which it is impossible to employ as it is employing them without throwing to the winds all scruples of humanity or of respect for the understandings that were supposed to underlie the intercourse of the world.

I am not now thinking of the loss of property involved, immense and serious as that is, but only of the wanton and wholesale destruction of the lives of non-combatants, men, women and children, engaged in pursuits which have always, even in the darkest periods of modern history, been deemed innocent and legitimate. Property can be paid for; the lives of peaceful and innocent people cannot be.

German Warfare Is Against Mankind

The present German warfare against commerce is a warfare against mankind. It is a war against all nations. American ships have been sunk, American lives taken, in ways which it has stirred us very deeply to learn of, but the ships and people of other neutral and friendly nations have been sunk and overwhelmed in the waters in the same way. There has been no discrimination. The challenge is to all mankind. Each nation must decide for itself how it will meet it. The choice we make for ourselves must be made with a moderation of counsel and a temperateness of judgment befitting our character and our motives as a nation. We must put excited feeling away. Our motive will not be revenge or the victorious assertion of the physical might of the nation, but only the vindication of right, of human right, of which we are only a single champion.

It Now Appears Armed Neutrality Is Impracticable

When I addressed the Congress on the twenty-sixth of February last I thought that it would suffice to assert our neutral rights with arms, our right to use the seas against unlawful interference, our right to keep our people safe against unlawful violence. But armed neutrality, it now appears, is impracticable.

Because submarines are in effect outlaws when used as the German submarines have been used, against merchant shipping, it is impossible to defend ships against their attacks, as the law of nations has assumed that merchantmen would defend themselves against privateers or cruisers, visible craft giving chase upon the open sea. It is common prudence in such circumstances, —grim necessity, indeed—to endeavor to destroy them before they have shewn their own intention. They must be dealt with upon sight, if dealt with at all.

The German government denies the right of neutrals to use arms at all within the areas of the sea which it has proscribed, even in the defence of rights which no modern publicist has ever before questioned their right to defend. The intimation is conveyed that the armed guards which we have placed on our merchant ships will be treated as beyond the pale of law and subject to be dealt with as pirates would be.

Armed neutrality is ineffectual enough at best; in such circumstances and in the face of such pretensions it is worse than ineffectual; it is likely to produce what it was meant to prevent; it is practically certain to draw us into the war without either the rights or the effectiveness of belligerents.

There Is One Choice We Cannot Make

There is one choice we cannot make, we are incapable of making: We will not choose the path of submission and suffer the most sacred rights of our nation and our people to be ignored or violated. The wrongs against which we now array ourselves are not common wrongs; they cut to the very roots of human life.

In Fact Nothing Less Than War

With a profound sense of the solemn and even tragical character of the step I am taking and of the grave responsibilities which it involves, but in unhesitating obedience to what I deem my constitutional duty, I advise that the Congress declare the recent course of the Imperial German Government to be in fact nothing less than war against the government and people of the United States; that it formally accept the status of belligerent which has thus been thrust upon it, and that it take immediate steps not only to put the country in a more thorough state of defence, but also to exert all its power and employ all its resources to bring the government of the German Empire to terms and end the war.

What This Will Involve Is Clear

What this will involve is clear. It will involve the utmost practicable coöperation in counsel and action with the governments now at war with Germany, and, as incident to that, the extension to those governments of the most liberal financial credits in order that our resources may, so far as possible, be added to theirs.

It will involve the organization and mobilization of all the material resources of the country to supply the materials of war and serve the incidental needs of the nation in the most abundant and yet the most economical and efficient way possible.

It will involve the immediate full equipment of the navy in all respects, but particularly in supplying it with the best means of dealing with the enemy's submarines. It will involve the immediate addition to the armed forces of the United States, already provided for by law in case of war, at least 500,000 men, who should, in my opinion, be chosen upon the principle of universal liability to service; and also the authorization of subsequent additional increments of equal force so soon as they may be needed and can be handled in training.

It will involve also, of course, the granting of adequate credits to the government, sustained, I hope, so far as they can equitably be sustained by the present generation, by well conceived taxation. I say sustained so far as may be by equitable taxation because it seems to me that it would be most unwise to base the credits which will now be necessary entirely on money borrowed. It is our duty, I most respectfully urge, to protect our people so far as we may against the very serious hardships and evils which would be likely to arise out of the inflation which would be produced by vast loans.

Must Not Interfere With Allied Munitions

In carrying out the measures by which these things are to be accomplished we should keep constantly in mind the wisdom of interfering as little as possible in our own preparation and in the equipment of our own military forces with the duty —for it will be a very practical duty—of supplying the nations already at war with Germany with the materials which they can obtain only from us or by our assistance. They are in the field, and we should help them in every way to be effective there.

I shall take the liberty of suggesting, through the several executive departments of the government, for the consideration of your committees measures for the accomplishment of the several objects I have mentioned. I hope that it will be your pleasure to deal with them as having been framed after very careful thought by the branch of the government upon which the responsibility of conducting the war and safeguarding the nation will most directly fall.

While We Do These Things

While we do these things, these deeply momentous things, let us be very clear, and make very clear to all the world what our motives and our objects are. My own thought has not been driven from its habitual and normal course by the unhappy events of the last two months, and I do not believe that the thought of the nation has been altered or clouded by them.

I have exactly the same thing in mind now that I had in mind when I addressed the Senate on the 22d of January last; the same that I had in mind when I addressed the Congress on the 3d of February and on the 26th of February. Our object now, as then, is to vindicate the principles of peace and the justice in the life of the world as against selfish and autocratic power and to set up among the really free and self-governed peoples of the world such a concert of purpose and of action as will henceforth insure the observance of those principles.

One Morality for Nations and Persons

Neutrality is no longer feasible or desirable where the peace of the world is involved and the freedom of its peoples, and the menace to that peace and freedom lies in the existence of autocratic governments backed by organized force which is controlled wholly by their will, not by the will of their people. We have seen the last of neutrality in such circumstances.

We are at the beginning of an age in which it will be insisted that the same standards of conduct and of responsibility for wrong done shall be observed among nations and their governments that are observed among the individual citizens of civilized states.

We Have No Quarrel With the German People

We have no quarrel with the German people. We have no feeling toward them but one of sympathy and friendship. It was not upon their impulse that their government acted in entering this war. It was not with their previous knowledge or approval.

It was a war determined upon as wars used to be determined upon in the old unhappy days when peoples were nowhere consulted by their rulers and wars were provoked and waged in the interest of dynasties or of little groups of ambitious men who were accustomed to use their fellowmen as pawns and tools.

Self-governed nations do not fill their neighbor states with spies or set the course of intrigue to bring about some critical posture of affairs which will give them an opportunity to strike and make conquest. Such designs can be successfully worked only under cover and where no one has the right to ask questions.

Cunningly contrived plans of deception or aggression, carried, it may be, from generation to generation, can be worked out and kept from the light only within the privacy of courts or behind the carefully guarded confidences of a narrow and privileged class. They are happily impossible where public opinion commands and insists upon full information concerning all the nation's affairs.

It Must Be A League of Honor

A steadfast concert for peace can never be maintained except by a partnership of democratic nations. No autocratic government could be trusted to keep faith within it or observe its covenants.

It must be a league of honor, a partnership of opinion. Intrigue would eat its vitals away; the plottings of inner circles who could plan what they would and render account to no one would be a corruption seated at its very heart.

Only free peoples can hold their purpose and their honor steady to a common end and prefer the interests of mankind to any narrow interest of their own.

Here Is a Fit Partner

Does not every American feel that assurance has been added to our hope for the future peace of the world by the wonderful and heartening things that have been happening within the last few weeks in Russia?

Russia was known by those who knew it best to have been always in fact democratic at heart, in all the vital habits of her thought, in all the intimate relationships of her people that spoke for their natural instinct, their habitual attitude toward life.

Autocracy that crowned the summit of her political structure, long as it had stood and terrible as was the reality of its power, was not in fact Russian in origin, in character or purpose, and now it has been shaken, and the great, generous Russian people have been added in all their native majesty and might to the forces that are fighting for freedom in the world, for justice and for peace. Here is a fit partner for a league of honor.

Spies Were Here Before the War Began

One of the things that have served to convince us that the Prussian autocracy was not and could never be our friend is that from the very outset of the present war it has filled our unsuspecting communities and even our offices of government with spies and set criminal intrigues everywhere afoot against our national unity of council, our peace within and without, our industries and our commerce.

Indeed, it is now evident that its spies were here even before the war began; and it is unhappily not a matter of conjecture, but a fact proved in our courts of justice, that the intrigues, which have more than once come perilously near to disturbing the peace and dislocating the industries of the country, have been carried on at the instigation, with the support, and even under the personal direction, of official agents of the imperial government accredited to the government of the United States.

Even in checking these things and trying to extirpate them we have sought to put the most generous interpretation possible upon them, because we knew that their source lay, not in any hostile feeling or purpose of the German people toward us (who were, no doubt, as ignorant of them as we ourselves were), but only in the selfish designs of a government that did what it pleased and told its people nothing. But they have played their part in serving to convince us at last that that government entertains no real friendship for us, and means to act against our peace and security at its convenience.

For the Ultimate Peace of the World

That it means to stir up enemies against us at our very doors the intercepted note to the German Minister at Mexico City is eloquent evidence.

We are accepting this challenge of hostile purpose because we know that in such a government, following such methods, we can never have a friend, and that in the presence of its organized power, always lying in wait to accomplish we know not what purpose, there can be no assured security for the democratic governments of the world.

We are now about to accept gage of battle with this natural foe to liberty and shall, if necessary, spend the whole force of the nation to check and nullify its pretensions and its power. We are glad, now that we see the facts with no veil of false pretence about them, to fight thus for the ultimate peace of the world and for the liberation of its peoples, the German peoples included, for the rights of nations great and small, and the privilege of men everywhere to choose their way of life and of obedience.

The world must be made safe for democracy. Its peace must be planted upon the trusted foundations of political liberty.

We have no selfish ends to serve. We desire no conquest, no dominion. We seek no indemnities for ourselves, no material compensation for the sacrifices we shall freely make. We are but one of the champions of the rights of mankind. We shall be satisfied when those rights have been as secure as the faith and the freedom of the nation can make them.

Just because we fight without rancor and without selfish objects, seeking nothing for ourselves but what we shall wish to share with all free peoples, we shall, I feel confident, conduct our operations as belligerents without passion and ourselves observe with proud punctilio the principles of right and of fair play we profess to be fighting for.

Will Deal with Austria Later

I have said nothing of the governments allied with the imperial government of Germany, because they have not made war upon us or challenged us to defend our right and our honor. The Austro-Hungarian government has, indeed, avowed its unqualified indorsement and acceptance of the reckless and lawless submarine warfare adopted now without disguise by the imperial government, and it has therefore not been possible for this government to receive Count Tarnowski, the ambassador recently accredited to this government by the imperial and royal government of Austria-Hungary, but that government has not actually engaged in warfare against citizens of the United States on the seas, and I take the liberty, for the present at least, of postponing a discussion of our relations with the authorities at Vienna. We enter this war only where we are clearly forced into it because there are no other means of defending our rights.

Because We Act Without Animus

It will be all the easier for us to conduct ourselves as belligerents in a high spirit of right and fairness because we act without animus, not in enmity toward a people or with the desire to bring any injury or disadvantage upon them, but only in armed opposition to an irresponsible government which has thrown aside all considerations of humanity and of right and is running amuck.

We are, let me say again, the sincere friends of the German people, and shall desire nothing so much as the early reëstablishment of intimate relations of mutual advantage between us—however hard it may be for them, for the time being, to believe that this is spoken from our hearts. We have borne with their present government through all these bitter months because of that friendship—exercising a patience and forbearance which would otherwise have been impossible.

The Millions of German Birth Who Live Among Us

We shall, happily, still have an opportunity to prove that friendship in our daily attitude and actions toward the millions of men and women of German birth and native sympathy who live amongst us and share our life, and we shall be proud to prove it toward all who are in fact loyal to their neighbors and to the government in the hour of test. They are, most of them, as true and loyal Americans as if they had never known any other fealty or allegiance. They will be prompt to stand with us in rebuking and restraining the few who may be of a different mind and purpose.

If There Should Be Disloyalty

If there should be disloyalty it will be dealt with with a firm hand of stern repression; but if it lifts its head at all, it will lift it only here and there, and without countenance, except from a lawless and malignant few.

It is a distressing and oppressive duty, gentlemen of the Congress, which I have performed in thus addressing you. There are, it may be, many months of fiery trial and sacrifice ahead of us. It is a fearful thing to lead this great peaceful people into war, into the most terrible and disastrous of all wars, civilization itself seeming to be in the balance.

But the right is more precious than peace, and we shall fight for the things which we have always carried nearest our hearts—for democracy, for the right of those who submit to authority to have a voice in their own governments, for the rights and liberties of small nations, for a universal dominion of right by such a concert of free peoples as shall bring peace and safety to all nations and make the world itself at last free.

Privileged to Spend Her Blood

To such a task we can dedicate our lives and our fortunes, everything that we are and everything that we have, with the pride of those who knew that the day has come when America is privileged to spend her blood and her might for the principles that gave her birth and happiness and the peace which she has treasured. God helping her, she can do no other.

Wilson's Plan Provides for Full Warfare

Universal Service; a First Army of 500,000 Men at Once; Liberal Loans to Europe

Congress May Act To-day

President Urges Utmost Practical Co-operation with Governments at War with Germany

(By Associated Press)

Washington, April 2.—Immediately after the President ended his message to Congress urging war the following joint resolution was introduced in both the Senate and House and referred to committee:

Joint resolution declaring that a state of war exists between the imperial German government and the government and people of the United States and making provision to prosecute the same:

Whereas, The recent acts of the imperial government are acts of war against the government and people of the United States;

Resolved, by the Senate and House of Representatives of the United States of America in Congress assembled, That the state of war between the United States and the imperial German government which has been thus thrust upon the United States is hereby formally declared; and

That the President be, and he is hereby, authorized and directed to take immediate steps not only to put the country in a thorough state of defence, but also to exert all of its power and employ all of its resources to carry on war against the imperial German government and to bring the conflict to a successful termination.

"War" Committee Will Meet To-day

Washington, April 2.—Chairman Stone of the Senate Foreign Relations Committee, which would handle any resolution declaring war or a state of war, late to-day called a meeting of his committee for 10 o'clock to-morrow morning.

"I am against a declaration of war," he added, "but when it is declared I will be a war eagle screaming as loud as the rest. Blood is thicker than water, and no matter what opinions a man might have about the need for war, any other position would be contemptible, and no American could contemplate it.

"War is not play, and when we go into it I believe we should go in to the limit with men and money. If it takes one million men, all right; if it takes five million men, all right; if it takes ten billion dollars or fifty billion dollars, all right. There is no use playing around the edges of war."

Washington, April 2.—President Wilson to-night urged Congress, assembled in joint session, to declare that a state of war exists between the United States and Germany.

When the President had finished speaking, resolutions to declare a state of war existing and to direct him to exert all the power of the United States against Germany were introduced in both houses of Congress, referred to appropriate committees and will be debated to-morrow. There is no doubt of their passage.

Destroy Autocratic Rule in Germany

The United States must enter the war, the President said, to make the world safe for democracy. He declared that the aim of this nation was to free the German people from their autocratic rulers.

The President's address was sent in full to Germany by a German official news agency for publication in that country. The text also went to England, and a summary of its contents was sent around the world to other nations.

Wilson's Programme of Action in War

To carry on an effective war the President recommended:

Utmost practical coöperation in counsel and action with the governments already at war with Germany.

Extension of liberal financial credits to those governments so that the resources of America may be added so far as possible to theirs.

Organization and mobilization of all the material resources of the country.

Full equipment of the navy, particularly for means of dealing with submarine warfare.

An army of at least 500,000 men, based on the principle of universal liability to service, and the authorization of additional increments of 500,000 each as they are needed or can be handled in training.

Raising necessary money for the United States government, so far as possible without borrowing, and on the basis of equitable taxation.

All preparations, the President urged, should be made in such a way as not to check the flow of war supplies to the nations already in the field against Germany.

Measures to acomplish all these

THE SECOND DAY

Uncertain Trumpets

TUESDAY, APRIL 3, dawned generally fair throughout the United States. All across the country the press gave, of course, full coverage to the President's message and its delivery. Editorial comment predominantly approved. The gamut ran from the Los Angeles *Times'* "we accept the challenge of a hostile purpose," to the New York *Tribune's* "no praise can be too high. . . . We are done with the doctrine of 'too proud to fight'."

Below banner headlines the New York *Herald* inserted in its running front-page account a three-column box, enclosing Julia Ward Howe's "Battle Hymn of the Republic." But in Emporia, Kansas, William Allen White's *Gazette* thrilled its readers with a hysterical editorial, ending on a gory "bloodshed in a holy cause" note diametrically opposed to Mr. Wilson's lament of the previous night.

The New York *Call,* recalcitrant exception, snarled bitterly: "This country is divided into two camps—Americans and militarists." But the German-American press in the main followed the *New Yorker Staats Zeitung's* flat pronouncement: "The President need have no concern as to the loyalty of Americans of German descent." All the German-American newspapers noted that Mr. Wilson had specifically directed his enmity toward the Kaiser and his government, not the German people.

German-Americans in an Albany, New York, brewery mobbed an Austrian fellow-employee who refused to salute the American flag. A German-American mass meeting in San Jose, California, while declaring loyalty to the United States, recommended a national referendum on a war declaration—a course previously urged by German sympathizers in Wisconsin and in Congress.

Irish-American voices denouncing England were muted in the Hearst newspapers, and McCormick's Chicago *Tribune,* also pro-Irish in sentiment, forgot the Sinn Fein rebellion in Dublin and its drastic suppression by the British. The hyphens were sloughing off.

The press united in prediction that a declaration of war would slide

*Following a guerilla attack on a New Mexican village by the
Mexican bandit, Pancho Villa, President Wilson ordered a
punitive expedition of 5,000 Army Regulars sent in pursuit
of Villa into Mexico. This action eventually led to the
mobilization of the National Guard and the dispatch of 130,000
Regulars along the Mexican border. These men are troops of
the 11th Cavalry moving south in Mexico near Casas Grande.*

through the Congress this day, without hitch. So once again public
interest focused on Washington, where the Congressional wheels were
beginning to turn.

The Senate, after ridding itself of a vast accumulation of reports
from constituents that would end up in 24 pages of small type in the

Congressional Record, turned to the business of the day. Senator Gilbert M. Hitchcock of Nebraska read the joint resolution drafted in the House Foreign Affairs Committee the previous night and approved in his Senate Foreign Relations Committee earlier in the morning. Hitchcock was acting in place of the committee chairman, Senator William J. Stone, who had cast one lone vote of dissent to the paper.

> "Whereas the recent acts of the Imperial German Government are acts of war against the government and people of the United States, resolved by the Senate and House of Representatives of the United States of America in Congress assembled, that the state of war between the United States and the Imperial German Government, which has been thrust

The Chicago Daily Tribune.

THE WORLD'S GREATEST NEWSPAPER

FINAL EDITION

XVI.—NO. 80. C. BY THE TRIBUNE COMPANY.] TUESDAY, APRIL 3, 1917.—TWENTY-FOUR PAGES. ✳ ✳ PRICE ONE CENT.

S. AT WAR: WILSON

NOW FOR THE DEEDS

[Copyright: 1917: by John T. McCutcheon.]

WARNINGS TO GERMANY!

WORDS WORDS WORDS
WORDS WORDS
WORDS WORDS
WORDS WORDS
WORDS WORDS
WORDS
WORDS
WORDS
ORDS
WORDS
ORDS
WORDS
WORDS
ORDS
WORDS WORDS
WORDS WORDS
ORDS WORDS WAR
WORDS WO

DEEDS

THE WEATHER.

TUESDAY, APRIL 3, 1917.

Sunrise, 5:29; sunset, 6:17. Moon sets at 0:55 a. m.

Chicago and vicinity:—Increasing cloudiness Tuesday, followed by rain Tuesday night and Wednesday. Cooler Wednesday; Winds becoming fresh and southeast.

Illinois — Increasing cloudiness and somewhat warmer Tuesday, followed by rain Tuesday night and Wednesday. Cooler Wednesday.

TEMPERATURE IN CHICAGO.
[Last 24 hours.]

Maximum, 51 a. m.....44
Minimum, 36 a. m.....37

8 a. m.....40	7 p. m.....40
9 a. m.....41	8 p. m.....39
10 a. m.....41	9 p. m.....40
11 a. m.....44	10 p. m.....39
12 m.....44	11 p. m.....39
1 p. m.....44	12 Midnight...38
2 p. m.....44	1 a. m.....38
3 p. m.....41	2 a. m.....38

Mean temperature, 40; normal for the day, 41. Deficiency since Jan. 1, 1.
Precipitation for 24 hours to 7 p. m...00. Deficiency since Jan. 1, 2.59 inches.
Wind, N.; maximum velocity, 20 miles an hour, at 10:41 p. m.

For complete weather report see page 18.

YESTERDAY ELSEWHERE.

	Temp.		
	High.	Low.	
New York...60	40	40	Clear
Boston........56	40	38	Rain
Washington....60	40	40	Clear
St. Louis......60	50	28	Clear
St. Paul.......44	44	28	Fair
San Francisco...58	56	46	Clear

SUMMARY OF THE WAR

London reports capture of more French villages and German trenches on a ten mile front. New only two miles from St. Quentin. French continue advance and Germans admit retreat at various points.

DEFENSE BODY LAYS PLANS FOR 3 YEARS OF WAR

Washington, D. C., April 2—Samuel Gompers and Howard E. Coffin, members of the advisory commission of the national council of defense, think the war may last three years. They are here attending a meeting of the committee on labor.

Mr. Gompers is chairman. One hundred and twenty-five of the leading labor men, physicians, scientists, and sociologists of the United States attended. Secretary of Labor Wilson spoke.

The meeting was to form subordinate committees to take up universal service. Mr. Gompers pointed out England's war plans are for two more years of war.

Mr. Coffin said:

"Every plan which we lay down will be on a basis of three years of warfare. We are entering upon the greatest period of universal service in the history of the world."

REPORTS MEXICO PLANS TO LEASE ISLAND TO JAPAN

Los Angeles, Cal., April 2—[Special.]—The Mexican government, through José Valjardi, minister of mines, is negotiating with a Japanese syndicate which seeks a long term fishing lease of the island of Tibureon in the Gulf of California, according to Robert L. Hogue, a mining engineer of Los Angeles and Antonio, who has just arrived here from Mexico.

Hogue says he learned of the proposed deal while in Mexico three weeks ago when he was called on by Valjardi for an opinion concerning the mineral value of the island and was told that a deal was about

---

VOTE TODAY! CITY ELECTION

Polls open from 6 a. m. to 4 p. m. Women have equal voting rights with men on all candidates and on the five bond issues.

THE TRIBUNE recommendations to voters are as follows:

For City Clerk—JAMES T. IGOE. Dem.

For City Treasurer—JAMES J. CULLEN, Rep.

FOR ALDERMEN

Ward.
1—FRED E. WENIG, Dem.
2—GEORGE F. ILIFF, Dem.
3—JOSEPH B. McDONOUGH, Rep.
4—ALEXANDER A. McCORMICK, Rep.
5—WILLIAM N. FETZER, Rep.
6—JOHN R. TYDEN, Rep.
7—HIRAM VANDERBILT, Rep.
8—OTTO KERNER, Dem.
9—JOHN B. ANDERSON, Rep.
10—GEORGE M. MAYPOLE, Dem.
11—JOHN J. TOUHY, Ind. Rep.
12—ROBERT H. McCORMICK, Rep.
13—THOMAS O. WALLACE, Rep.
(WALTER F. STEFFEN, Rep.)
14—HERMAN E. GNADT, Rep.
25—HENRY D. CAPITAIN, Dem.
26—WILLIAM F. LIPPS, Rep.
28—JAMES M. McFARLAND, Rep.
33—HARRY E. LITTLER, Dem.
30—JAMES A. HASTINGS, Rep.
32—JAMES A. LONG, Dem.
33—A. J. FISHER, Rep.
35—DELTA I. JARRETT, Dem.
35—JOHN S. CLARK, Dem.

*Full term. †Short term.

THE TRIBUNE advises voters to support all of the bond propositions.

"No War" Messages Load the Wires to Washington

BOTH HOUSES HASTEN WORK ON PROGRAM

Resolution Will Be Passed at Once—Universal Service Aided.

BY ARTHUR SEARS HENNING.

Washington, D. C., April 2.—[Special.]—Amid demonstrations of tumultuous enthusiasm such as seldom has been seen at the national capitol, President Wilson asked congress tonight to declare the existence of a state of war with Germany, brought about by the acts of the Berlin government.

Immediately after the president left the capitol the senate and house reconvened and an identic joint resolution—drawn by the president—was introduced in both houses, declaring the existence of a state of war and directing the president to employ all the resources of the country to carry on war against the imperial German government and "bring the conflict to a successful conclusion."

SENT TO COMMITTEES.

The resolution was introduced in the senate by Senator Martin of Virginia. Representative Flood, chairman of the house foreign affairs committee, introduced it in the house.

The resolution was referred to the foreign affairs committees by both houses, and approval presumably will follow soon afterward.

Senate administration leaders planned to have the foreign relations committee report the war resolution to the senate tomorrow morning. Senator Hitchcock, ranking Democrat of the committee, probably will manage the debate as the spokesman for the majority, as Senator Stone of Missouri, chairman, has announced his opposition to the measure.

Prompt action also is expected of the house committee and debate in the house under a special rule limiting debate may begin there tomorrow afternoon.

Congress, according to indications tonight, will adopt the resolution by an overwhelming majority.

FOR UNIVERSAL SERVICE.

The feature of the president's war program which aroused the most discussion was that in which he referred to the raising of an army in these words:

"It will involve the immediate addition to the armed force of the United States already provided for by law in case of war at least 500,000 men, who should, in my opinion, be chosen upon the principle of universal liability to service, and also the authorization of subsequent additional increments of equal force so soon as they may be needed and can be handled in training."

Military authorities regard this as an unqualified indorsement of universal service on the lines urged by the general staff of the army and exceeding even the measures urged by Senator Chamberlain, of the military affairs committee.

GIVES SCATHING INDICTMENT.

In the address the president delivered a scathing indictment of the German government, not only for responsibility for the ruthless submarine warfare to which 250 American lives have been sacrificed, but for the plots and other acts of hostility against the United States.

Disclaiming any intention of warring upon the German people, for whom he said the United States will continue to manifest its warm regard, the executive appealed to the country to join the enente allies in crushing the autocratic imperial German government, characterized by the president as the implacable foe of democracy.

Confessing the failure and inade-

THE DECLARATION

A JOINT resolution prepared by the president and introduced last night in both houses of congress, and referred to the foreign affairs committee for consideration today, follows:

"Joint resolution declaring that a state of war exists between the imperial German government and the government and people of the United States and making provision to prosecute the same:

"Whereas, The recent acts of the imperial German government are acts of war against the government and people of the United States;

"Resolved, by the senate and house of representatives of the United States of America, in congress assembled, That the state of war between the United States and the imperial German government which has thus been thrust upon the United States is hereby formally declared; and

"That the president be and is hereby authorized and directed to take immediate steps not only to put the country in a thorough state of defense but also to exert all of its power and employ all of its resources to carry on war against the imperial German government and to bring the conflict to a successful termination."

THE WAR PLAN

PRESIDENT WILSON'S address to congress last night told what the war program of the United States will be. On this Mr. Wilson said:

It will involve the utmost practicable co-operation in counsel and action with the governments now at war with Germany and, as incident to that, the extension to those governments of the most liberal credit, in order that our resources may be added to theirs.

RESOURCES.

It will involve the organization and mobilization of all the material resources of the country to supply the materials of war and serve the incidental needs of the nation in the most abundant and yet the most economical and efficient way possible.

THE NAVY.

It will involve the immediate full equipment of the navy in all respects, but particularly in supplying it with the best means of dealing with the enemy's submarines.

THE ARMY.

It will involve the immediate addition to the armed forces of the United States already provided for by law in case of war at least 500,000 men, who should, in my opinion, be chosen upon the principle of universal liability to service, and also the authorization of subsequent additional increments of equal force so soon as they may be needed and can be handled in training.

FINANCE.

It will involve the granting of adequate credits to the government, sustained, I hope, so far as they can equitably be sustained by the present generation, by well conceived taxation. . . . It seems to me that it would be most unwise to base the credits which will now be necessary entered on borrowed money.

MUNITIONS.

We should interfere as little as possible . . . with the duty for it will be a very practical duty—of supplying the nations already at war with Germany with the material which they can obtain only from us.

COLT ARMS CUTS $2,500,000 MELON

Hartford, Conn., April 2—[Special.]—At the annual meeting today of the stockholders of the Colt Patent Firearms Manufacturing company a $2,500,000

"WE MUST FIGHT FOR JUSTICE AND RIGHTS"

President Tells Joint Session of Congress That German Monarchy Is Threat to All Mankind.

WASHINGTON, D. C., April 2.—(Special.)—President Wilson's epochal address to congress, calling for action against Germany, delivered tonight, follows:

"Gentlemen of the Congress: I have called the congress into extraordinary session because there are serious, very serious, choices of policy to be made, and made immediately, which it is neither right nor constitutionally permissible that I should assume the responsibility of making.

"On the 3d of February last I officially laid before you the extraordinary announcement of the imperial German government that on and after the first day of February it was its purpose to put aside all restraints of law or of humanity and use its submarines to sink every vessel that sought to approach either the ports of Great Britain and Ireland or the western coast of Europe or any of the ports controlled by the enemies of Germany within the Mediterranean.

HOPED FOR MODIFIED WARFARE.

"That had seemed to be the object of the German submarine warfare earlier in the war, but since April of last year the imperial government had somewhat restrained the commanders of its undersea craft in conformity with its promise then given to us that passenger boats should not be sunk and that due warning would be given to all other vessels which its submarines might seek to destroy, when no resistance was offered or escape attempted, and care taken that their crews were given at least a fair chance to save their lives in their open boats.

"The precautions taken were meager and haphazard enough, as was proved in distressing instance after instance in the progress of the cruel and unmanly business, but a certain degree of restraint was observed.

"The new policy has swept every restriction aside. Vessels of every kind, whatever their flag, their character, their cargo, their destination, their errand, have been ruthlessly sent to the bottom without warning and without thought of help or mercy for those on board, the vessels of friendly neutrals along with those of belligerents.

"Even hospital ships and ships carrying relief to the sorely bereaved and stricken people of Belgium, though the latter were provided with safe conduct through the proscribed area by the German government itself and were distinguished by unmistakable marks of identity, have been sunk with the same reckless lack of compassion or of principle.

RELIED ON LAW OF NATIONS.

"I was for a little while unable to believe that such things would be in fact done by any government that had hitherto subscribed to the humane practices of civilized nations.

"International law had its origin in the attempt to set up some law which would be respected and observed upon the seas, where no nation had right of dominion and where lay the free highways of the world. By painful stage after stage had that law been built up, with meager enough results, indeed, after all was accomplished that could be accomplished, but always with a clear view, at least, of what the heart and conscience of mankind demanded.

"This minimum of right the German government has swept aside under the plea of retaliation and necessity and because it had no weapons which it could use at sea except these which it is impossible to employ as it is employing them without throwing to the winds all scruples of humanity or of respect for the understandings that were supposed to underlie the intercourse of the world.

CHALLENGE TO ALL MANKIND.

"I am not now thinking of the loss of property involved, immense and serious as that is, but only of the wanton and wholesale destruction of the lives of noncombatants, men, women, and children, engaged in pursuits which have always, even in the darkest periods of modern history, been deemed innocent and legitimate. Property can be paid for; the lives of peaceful and innocent people cannot be. The present German submarine warfare against commerce is a warfare against mankind.

"It is a war against all nations. American ships have been sunk, American lives taken, in ways which it has stirred us very deeply to learn of, but the ships and people of other neutral and friendly nations have been sunk and overwhelmed in the waters in the same way.

"There has been no discrimination. The challenge is to all mankind. Each nation must decide for itself how it will meet it. The choice we make for ourselves must be made with a moderation of counsel and a temperateness of judgment befitting our character and our motives as a nation. We must not excited feelings away. Our motive will not be re-

upon the United States, is hereby formally declared; and that the President be and he is hereby, authorized and directed to take immediate steps, not only to put the country in a thorough state of defense, but also to exert all its power and employ all of its resources to carry on war against the Imperial German Government and to bring the conflict to a successful conclusion."

His recitation concluded, Hitchcock asked unanimous consent for immediate consideration. It was in the bag, it seemed, and in the press gallery reporters reached to scribble flashes. But their pencils halted as Senator La Follette brought the war-making machinery to a grinding stop.

"I object to the request for unanimous consideration!"

The subject must, he added, go over for the day, under the usual rules of Senate procedure. And he cut short the babble of expostulation with

(Right) To Major Enoch H. Crowder, later a Major General, the General Staff gave the task of developing a universal military draft system acceptable to the American people.

(Left) The morning after the President's call for war, the ultra-neutralist Chicago Tribune came out in support of Wilson and his war policy.

Alvin C. York was a Tennesee farmer and blacksmith when the
war began. He was raised in the Fundamentalist belief,
"Thou shalt not kill." Caught in the draft, P.F.C. York,
18 months later, convinced he could kill in defense of his
country, single-handedly stormed an enemy machine gun nest, shot
down 15 of the foe and took 132 prisoners and several guns.
For his exploit he won the Medal of Honor and immortal fame.

As the war began, Major Douglas MacArthur was serving
War Secretary Newton D. Baker as the War Department censor
and information officer in Washington. Later, he was picked by
Baker to become Chief of Staff of the 42nd "Rainbow"
Division, the National Guard's first unit overseas.
Dashing and daring, the young Major rose
to become a Brigadier General by the war's end.

what one reporter termed "sarcastic emphasis": "I have asked for the regular order, and I ask for a ruling upon that request."

That was that. The reporters could and did scrawl flashes now, but of entirely different tenor. For under the Senate rules La Follette was right. There could be no further comment, no further discussion today. So the resolution was laid aside, the baffled Senate adjourned until the following morning, and its leaders, faced by the promise of another La Follette filibuster, went into immediate huddle to arrange for a new cloture rule and continuous session.

But if the Congressional machinery hung momentarily on dead center this brisk, sunny morning, things were bustling at the other end of Pennsylvania Avenue. The massive State, War and Navy Building rocked with the efforts of the service departments to overcome a long-time lag.

From elderly Major General Hugh L. Scott, chief of staff, a short-spoken man whose conversations were always elaborated by a flurry of Indian sign-language, down to the newest messenger, the War Department was wrestling with an unprecedented expansion program.

The 130,000 Regulars were mostly still dispersed along the Mexican border. Some 50,000 National Guardsmen, a quarter of the citizen-soldiers who had just come back from the Rio Grande, were again in uniform, in small detachments guarding bridges and other sensitive points from a not entirely mythical threat of German sabotage. The officer corps, Regular and National Guard, totaled a mere 9,000-odd.

*Charles W. Whittlesey, a New York lawyer, gave up his practice
for a reserve commission. As commander of the 3rd Battalion,
308th Infantry—The Lost Battalion—Major Whittlesey
received the Medal of Honor for extricating his troops
from the German trap after five days of battle in the Argonne.*

Divisional and higher units did not exist. And now the President had
spoken of 500,000 men and more to come. Something had to be done,
and done fast.

The basic need, the most urgent and also the most sensitive, was for
manpower. The President's message, with its mention of universal service, awakened popular attention in a nation where "draft" had been a
dirty word since the Civil War, and recent War Department delibera-
tions on the subject had been shrouded in some secrecy.

All these things Scott knew this morning, as he had long known.
After all, his was the responsibility to make do in the national defense
with what the Congress provided. And this he had done by setting his
General Staff to work.

So, headed by slender Major Enoch H. Crowder, whose brilliant legal mind and high heart overcame the handicap of a frail constitution, a General Staff group was threshing out this morning one of the countless revisions of a plan destined to be acceptable to the American people. And in the office of War Secretary Baker a suave, tall, well-groomed major named Douglas MacArthur was deftly satisfying the queries of a rash of newspaper reporters and sugar-coating the pill of universal military service.

Down in the Tennessee mountains, some fifty or more miles north-west of Knoxville, in a Fentress County community bearing the incongruous name of Pall Mall, a twenty-nine-year-old, hickory-hard farmer-blacksmith was finishing his spring planting. He neither smoked,

General Pershing called Sam Woodfill, " the bravest man in the U.S. Army." A professional soldier all his life, Woodfill served as a sergeant with Pershing in Mexico. Two years later, wearing lieutenant bars, he won the Medal of Honor in France for single-handed silencing of four German machine gun nests.

Major General Leonard Wood, Medal of Honor winner,
Spanish-American War hero and father of the Plattsburg Idea—
a war preparedness plan for training civilian volunteers
for reserve commissions—was one of two ranking officers considered
to lead the American Expeditionary Force to Europe. General Wood,
however, had earned President Wilson's wrath due to his insistence
on preparedness in the face of the President's strong neutral stand.

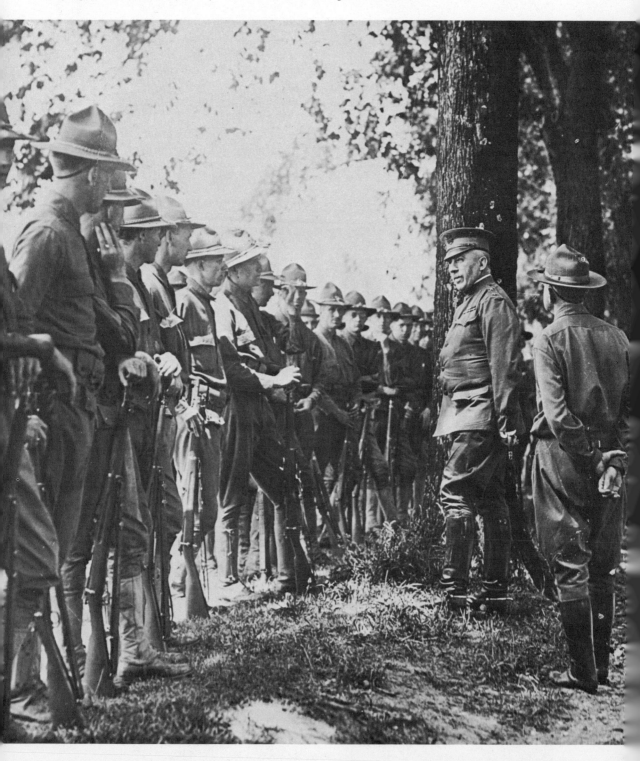

*When conscription was announced, Grover Cleveland Bergdoll,
together with his brother, both wealthy, spoiled sons of
German American parents, schemed how to dodge the draft.*

chewed, nor drank hard liquor. Like all his neighbors he had handled
a rifle since childhood and could pick off a squirrel or wild turkey like
nobody's business. Insofar as concerned relations with his fellow man,
a tenet of his stern Fundamentalist creed was "Thou shalt not kill." His
name was Alvin Cullum York, and he wouldn't learn of the doings up
in Washington for some time to come; news trickled but slowly into
"Parson" Pile's crossroads general store in Pall Mall, twenty miles from
railhead.

In his New York City office, a keen, thin, bespectacled young lawyer
who saw the handwriting on the wall was preparing to close down his
already lucrative practice. He was going home to his mother in Pitts-
field, Massachusetts, before cashing in his Plattsburg camp training of
1916 for a Reserve commission. His name was Charles W. Whittlesey.

*Among the many young men of substance and
standing who volunteered for military training
at Camp Plattsburg was Henry L. Stimson.*

On the Mexican border a stockily built professional soldier with
twenty years of hash marks, a sergeant's chevrons on his sleeve and a
heavy "sergeant major" mustache on his lip, was doing routine duty
with the 9th U.S. Infantry. Sam Woodfill expected that the 9th would
move overseas soon—wasn't that what the Regulars were for?—and
hoped that before he left he would be able to marry his long-time sweetheart.

Down on the border, too, at Leon Springs, Texas, a gregarious
twenty-nine year old first lieutenant and West Pointer, just returned
from a tour as inspector-instructor to militia, was taking up the prosaic
duties of regimental supply officer in the 19th Infantry. His name was
Dwight D. Eisenhower.

And at headquarters of the Western Department, in the Presidio of San Francisco, a taciturn captain of infantry who had entered the Regular Army via Virginia Military Institute was preparing to move to Governors Island, New York, with his chief, Major General J. Franklin Bell. Thirty-nine year old Captain George Catlett Marshall, Bell's aide, feared that the age and physical condition of his commander might be a bar to his own chances for overseas service.

In Philadelphia lived the American-born son of wealthy German-American parents whose assets came from the brewing business. For some unexplained reason he had been named after one of our most respected Presidents. This young man could fly a plane, could drive a racing car. He had more than once run afoul of the Philadelphia traffic

A soldier's soldier, Major General John Joseph (Blackjack) Pershing, seen here as a Brigadier General leading American regulars on their punitive expedition against Pancho Villa in Mexico, was a tough, stern, spit and polish cavalry officer. He was chosen over Gen. Leonard Wood by the President and War Secretary Baker to be commanding general of the future AEF.

The morning after the call to war, Bernard M. Baruch, a 37-year-old
financial wizard was enroute to Washington from New York
to join the National Security Council's advisory board.
With him, in front of the Treasury, is
Vance McCormick, publisher, industrialist and chairman of the War Trade Board.

police for reckless driving in city streets. He was the brattiest of spoiled brats, the apple of his Amazon mother's eye (his father was dead). Over the breakfast table this morning, with the bad news before them in the paper, he and his mother—who hated everything American—and his brother were planning how both young men could dodge the draft. His name was Grover Cleveland Bergdoll.

Two other men, long-time professional soldiers both, were scanning the news this morning. By coincidence, both were of the same age—57 years—and both wore two stars on their shoulder-straps. But one of them far outranked the other in grade. Major General Leonard Wood, Medal

Secretary of War Newton D. Baker was a quiet, strong-willed man, implicitly trusted by the President though virtually unknown by the public. He is seen pinning the Distinguished Service Medal on General Peyton C. March, Chief of Staff of the Army. At the time war was declared, March was only a major with the General Staff.

of Honor man and Spanish-American war hero, was father of the Platts-burg Idea—the voluntary civilian training which was already spawning the 96,000 reserve officers soon to make up forty-eight per cent of our final commissioned Army strength. This "Plattsburg Idea" had grown to include, besides young collegians, many men of substance and standing: among them New York City's young Mayor John Purroy Mitchel; war correspondent Richard Harding Davis; scions of the Chandler, Fish and Milburn clans; the young Roosevelts—Theodore, Jr., Kermit and Quentin; Robert C. Bacon; and Henry L. Stimson. General Wood was now in Charleston, South Carolina. Only a few weeks ago he had been transferred from Governors Island and the command of the Eastern Department because of his irrepressible insistence on preparedness. His active and dramatic cooperation in Theodore Roosevelt's attacks against the President's "vacillation" had earned Wilson's ire. Administration gossip had even said that Wood's personal supervision of a broomstick-armed group of volunteers training on Governors Island was a press-agent scheme. Wood well knew that a commander must soon be chosen for the expeditionary force envisioned in the President's war message. By rank, age and experience he would be the logical choice for the post, for fighting Frederick Funston, hero of the Philippine Insurrection and captor of Major General Emilio Aguinaldo, had died in February. But Wood today also knew that Presidents, like elephants, never forget. Only through some miracle could he expect to attain that coveted command.

The second man, a grim-faced cavalryman who had just proved in Mexico that come hell or high water he could obey to the letter the directive of a finicky commander-in-chief, sat close-mouthed at his desk in the headquarters of the Southern Department at Fort Sam Houston, San Antonio, Texas. He had just issued an order returning the last of the National Guard on the border to their home mobilization camps. He may or may not have known that the President and his Secretary of War had already made their choice for the new command, but the Regular Army freemasonry of this era was close-knit and its grapevine efficient. So it may be that Major General John Joseph Pershing was already planning in his mind the composition of the staff officers and principal unit commanders in his as yet nonexistent expeditionary force.

From the north and from the south two other men rode the rails to Washington this morning. Thirty-seven-year-old Bernard M. Baruch,

While Secretary of the Navy Josephus Daniels never achieved popularity among the old navy regulars, his assistant secretary, Franklin Delano Roosevelt, was very well-liked indeed. It was as a result of his war service that the young Roosevelt was able to build the foundation of his future political career.

already famed as a financial genius, was on the way from New York to join the advisory board of the President's National Security Council and to harness the nation's resources for war. And from Florida, where he had been stumping for preparedness, came former President Roosevelt of Spanish-American War fame breathing fire and brimstone. Toothy "T.R.," his long feud with Mr. Wilson momentarily forgotten, was racing to find out what the War Department had done with his latest scheme—the organization of a super-Rough Rider division, complete in horse, foot and guns, which he proposed to lead abroad in person. It was a dream he had harbored and fostered since the *Lusitania* went down.

Roosevelt's scheme had raised the hackles of the General Staff, for, if approved, it would upset ordered, intelligent Army-building. It would flout the concept of universal service by skimming the cream of prospective volunteers and, worse still, would bleed white the relatively small group of Regular officers on whom the entire proposed expansion must rest. For there was no doubt that "Teddy" would recruit his officers where he wished (doubtless with General Wood's advice and blessing). At the very least, creation of his proposed "elite" unit could wreck the morale of the whole.

All these objections were set down in the staff paper prepared by middle-aged, coldly efficient Major Peyton C. March and approved by the Chief of Staff. The paper lay on Mr. Baker's desk. So the Secretary of War was ready on that one.

The coming tussle with the ebullient Roosevelt was but one of the many problems that the efficient Baker was handling in his own quiet but incisive way. The man in the street didn't know much about Mr. Baker, who had come into office with the cachet of "pacifist" writ large upon him by the press. But Mr. Wilson knew him and trusted him. It was Baker's pressure that had converted the President to preparedness, and in this crisis Mr. Wilson was finding him a bulwark of sanity in a maelstrom of uncertainty and political self-seeking.

Nor did the man in the street know much about Baker's opposite number, Josephus Daniels, Secretary of the Navy, who also held court in the State, War and Navy Building. Daniels, the dean of Wilson's cabinet, was, in the public view, simply the man who created a Naval drought by banning hard liquor on board United States warships and in shore stations. The immediate reaction of the New York *Herald,* which rechristened the naval forces the "grapejuice Navy" and ham-

Press reaction to the President's war message was overwhelmingly favorable. The front page of the Washington Post *carried the full text of the President's message of the night before under banner headlines touching on the highlights of the speech. Also reported in detail was the sinking of the American steamer,* Aztec, *the first armed merchantman to have sailed from an American port.*

ANALYSIS DISCLOSES that [illegible] ...dally and [illegible] ...tration of the [illegible] constituency in Washington.

The Washington Post.

Weather—Fair and cooler today; tomorrow overcast and warmer, probably followed by rain. Temperature yesterday—Maximum, 80; minimum, 60.

...O. 14,903 — WASHINGTON: TUESDAY, APRIL 3, 1917.—FOURTEEN PAGES. — TWO CENTS.

...ERMANY MAKING WAR UPON U. S.; ACCEPT CHALLENGE OF NATURAL FOE TO LIBERTY WITH ALL OUR STRENGTH, PRESIDENT URGES CONGRESS

...ction by Congress in Response to the President's Appeal Is Assured; Country to Be at War Within a Few Days

President Wilson last night, amid scenes of tremendous patriotic enthusiam, asked Congress to declare that war ...ween the United States and Germany now exists and to take immediate steps, not only for a more through nat...al defense, but also "to exert all its power and employ all its resources to bring the Government of the German ...pire to terms and end the war." The President surprised many of his closest associates by proposing that a great force be raised for the principle of universal military service, starting with an army of 500,000 men.

...sident Wilson spoke as follows:

...ave called the Congress into extraordinary session because there are serious, very serious, ...es of policy to be made, and made immediatley, which it was neither right nor constitution...ermissible that I should assume the responsibility of making.

...the third of February last I officially laid before you teh extraordinary announcement of the ...ial German government that on and after the first day of February it was its purpose to ...side all restraints of law or of humanity and use its submarines to sink every vessel that ...t to approach either the ports of Great Btrain and Ireland or the western coasts of Eu...or any of the ports controlled by the enemies of Germany within the Mediterranean. That ...eemed to be the object of the German submarine warafre earlier in the war, but since ... of last year the imperial government had somewhat restrained the commanedrs of its ...sea craft in conformity with its promise then given to us that passenger boats should not ...k and that due warning would be given to all other vessel which its submarines might ...to destroy, when no resistance was offered or escape attempted, and care taken that their ... were given at least a fair chance to save their lives in their open boats.

Precautions Meager and Haphazard

...e precautions taken were meager and haphazard enough as was proved in distressing in...s in the progress of the cruel and unmanly buisness but a certain degree of restraint was ...ed.

...e new policy has swept every restriction aside. Vessels of every kind, whatever their flag, ...character, their cargo, their destination, their errand, have been ruthlessly sent to the bot...without warning, and without thought of help or mercy for those on board, the vessels of ...ly neutrals along with those of belligerents.

...r hospital ships and ships carrying relief to the so recently bereaved and stricken people ...lgium, though the latter were provided with safe conduct through the proscribed areas ...e German government itself and were distinguished by unmistakable marks of identity, ...been sunk with the same reckless lack of compassion or of principle.

...as for a little while unable to believe that such things would in fact be done by any govern... that had hitherto subscribed to the humane practices of civilized nations. International ...ad its origin in the attempt to set up some law which would be respected and observed ...the seas, where no nation had right of dominion and where lay the free highways of the

International Law Swept Aside

...painful stage after stage has that law been built up with meager enough results, indeed, ...all was accomplished that could be accomplished, but always with a clear view, at least, of ...the heart and conscience of mankind demanded. This minimum of right the German ...ment has swept aside under the plea of retaliation and necessity and because it had no ...ns which it could use at sea except these which it is impossible to employ as it is employing ...without throwing to the winds all scruples of humanity or of respect for the understand...hat were supposed to underlie the intercourse of the world.

...n not now thinking of the loss of property involved, immense and serious as that is, but ...f the wanton and wholesale destruction of the lives of noncombatants, men, women and ...n, engaged in pursuits which have always, even in the darkest periods of modern history, ...eemed innocent and legitimate.

...perty can be paid for; the lives of peaceful and innocent people cannot be. The present ...an submarine warfare against commerce is a warfare against mankind.

Germans Warring on All Nations

... a war against all nations. American ships have been sunk, American lives taken, in ...which it has stirred us very deeply to learn of, but the ships and people of other neutral ...s have been sunk and overwhelmed in the waters in the same way.

...re has been no discrimination. The challenge is to all mankind. Each nation must de...or itself how it will meet it. The choice we make for ourselves must be made with a mod... of counsel and a temperateness of judgment befitting our character and our motives ...ation. We must put excited feeling away. Our motive will not be revenge or the vic...s assertion of the physical might of the nation, but only the vindication of right, of human ...of which we are only a single champion.

...n I addressed the Congress on the twenty-sixth of February last I thought that it would ... to assert our neutarl rights with arms, our right to use the seas against unlawful inter...e, our right to keep our people safe against unlawful violence. But armed neutrality, it ...ppears, is impracticable.

Submarines in Effect Outlaws

...use submarines are in effect outalws when used as the German submarines have been ...gainst merchant shipping, it is impossible to defend ships against their attacks, as the ... nations has assumed that merchantmen would defend themselves against privateers or ...s, visible craft giving chase upon the open sea.

...s common prudence in such circumstances, grim necessity, indeed, to endeavor to destory ...before they have shown their own intention. They must be dealt with upon sight if dealt ...t all.

... German government denies the right of neutrals to use arms at all within the areas of the ...ich it has proscribed, even in the defense of rights which no modern publicist has ever be...uestioned their right to defend.

... intimation is conveyed that the armed guards which we have placed on our merchant ...will be treated as beyond the pale of law and subject to be dealt with as pirates would be.

...ed neutrality is ineffectual enough at best; in such circumstances and in the face of such ...ions it is worse than ineffectual; it is likely only to produce what it was meant to pre...t is practically certain to draw us into the war without either the rights or the effective...f belligerents.

Called War Against America

...e is one choice we cannot make, we are incapable of making: We will not choose the ...f submission and suffer the most sacred right sof our nation and our people to be ignored ...ated. The wrongs against which we now array ourselves are no common wrongs; they ...the very roots of human life.

... a profound sense of the solemn and even tragical characte rof the step I am taking and ...grave responsibilities which it involves, but in unhesitating obedience to what I deem my ...utional duty, I advise that the Congress declare the recent course of the imperial German ...ment to be in fact nothing less than war against the government and people of the ... States; that it formally accept the status of belligerency which has thus been thrust ... and that it take immediate steps not only to put the country in a more thorough state ...nse, but also to exert all its power and empoly all its resources to birng the government ...German empire to terms and end the war.

Financial Credits to the Allies

...t this will invoive is clear. It will involve the utmost practicable cooperation in counsel ...ion with the governments now at war with Germany and, as incident to that, the exten... those governments of the most liberal financial credits, in order that our resources may ...as possible be added to theirs.

...ill involve the organization and mobilization of all the material resources of the country ...ply the materials of war and serve the incidental needs of the nation in the most abundant ...t the most economical and efficient way possible. It will involve the immediate full ...ent of the navy in all respects, but particularly in supplying it with the best means of ... with the enemy's submarines.

...l involve the immediate additioo to the armed forces of the United States already pro...or by law in case of war at least 500,000 men, who should, in my opinion, be chosen upon ...nciple of universal liability to service, and also the authorization of subsequent additional ...ents of equal force so soon as they may be needed and can be handled in training.

...l involve also, of course, the granting of adequate credits to the government, sustained, I ...o far as they can equitably be sustained by the present generation, by well conceived ...n.

I say sustained so far as may be equitable by taxation because it seems to me that it would be most unwise to base the credits which will now be necessary entirely on money borrowed. It is our duty, I most respectfully urge, to protect our people so far as we may against the very serious hardships and evils which would be likely to arise out of the inflation which would be produced by vast loans.

In carrying out the measures by which these things are to be accomplished we should keep constantly in mind the wisdom of interfering as little as possible in our own preparation and in the equipment of our own military forces with the duty—for it will be a very practical duty—of supplying the nations already at war with Germany with the materials which they can obtain only from us or by our assistance. They are in the field and we should help them in every way to be effective there.

I shall take the liberty of suggesting, through the several executive departments of the government, for the consideration of you rcommittees, measures for the accomplishment of the several objects I have mentioned. I hope that it will be your pleasure to deal with them as having been framed after very careful thought by the branch of the government upon which the responsibility of conducting the war and safeguarding the nation will most directly fall.

While we do these things, these deeply momentous things, let us be very clear, and make very clear to al lthe world what our motives and our objects are. My own thought has not been driven from it shabitual and normal course by the unhappy events of the last two months, and I do not believe that the thought of the nation has been altered or clouded by them.

I have exactly the same things in mind now that I had in mind when I addresed the Senate on the 22d of January last; the same that I had in mind when I addressed the Congress on the 3d of February and on the 26th of February.

Our object now, as then, is to vindicate the principles of peace and justice in the life of the world as against selfish and autocratic power and to set up amongst the really free and self-governed peoples of the world such a concert of purpose and of action as will henceforth insure teh observance of those principles.

Neutrality is no longer feasible or desirable where the peace of the world is involved and the freedom of it speoples, and the menace to that peace and freedom lies in the existence of autocratic governments backed by organized force which is controlled wholly by their will, not by the will of their people. We have seen the last of neutrality in suc heircumstances.

We are at the beginning of an age in which it will be insisted that the same standards of conduct and responsibility for wrong done shall be observed among nations and their governments that are observed among the individual citizens of civilized states.

We have no quarrel with the German people. We have no feeling towards them but one of sympathy and friendship. It was not upon their impulse that their government acted in entering this war. It was not with their previous knowledge or approval. It was a war determined upon in the old, unhappy days when peoples were nowhere consulted by their rulers and wars were provoked and wagedi nthe interest of dynasties or of little groups of ambitious men who were accustomed to use their fellow men as pawns and tools.

Self-governed nations do not fill their neighbor states with spies or set the course of intrigue to bring about some critica lposture of affairs which will give them an opportunity to strike and make conquest. Such designs can be successfully worked out only under cover and where no one has the right to ask questions.

Cunningly contrived plans of deception or aggression, carried, it may be, from generation to generation, can be worked out and kept from the light only within the privacy of courts or behind the carefully guarded confidences of a narrow and privileged class. They are happily impossible where public opinion commands and insists upon full information concerning all the nation's affairs.

... steadfast concert for peace can never be maintained except by a partnership of democratic nations. No autocratic government could be trusted to keep faith within it or observe its covenants. It must be a league of honor, a partnership of opinion. Intrigue would eat its vitals away; the plottings of inner circles who could plan what they would and render account to no ... would be a corruption seated at its very heart.

Only free peoples can hold their purpose and their honor steady to a common end and prefer the interests of mankind to any narrow interest of their own.

Does not every American feel that assurance has been added to our hope for the future peace of the world by the wonderful and heartening things that have been happening within the last few weeks in Russia? Russia was known by those who knew it best to have been always in fact democratic at heart, in all the vital habits of her thought, in all the intimate relationships of her people that spoke their natural instinct, their habitual attitude towards life.

... autocracy that crowned the summit of hr political structure, long a sit had stood and terrible as was the reality of its power, was not in fact Russian in origin, character, or purpose; and now it has been shaken off and the great, generous Russian people have been added in all their naive majesty and might to the forces that are fighting for freedom in the world, for justice and for peace. Here is a fit partner for a league of honor.

One of the things that has served to convince us that the Prussian autocracy was not and could not never be our friend is that from the very outset of the present war it has filled our unsuspecting communities and even our offices of government with spies and set criminal intrigues everywhere afoot against our national unity of counsel, our peace within and without, our industries and our commerce.

Indeed, it is now evident that its spies were here even before the war began, and it is unhippaily not a matter of conjecture, but a fac proved in our courts of justice that the intrigues which have more than once come perilously near to disturbing the peace and dislocating the industries of the country have been carried on at the instigation, with the support, and even under the personal direction of official agents of the imperial government accredited to the government of the United States.

Even in checking these things and trying to extirpate them we have sought to put the most generous interpretation possible upon them because we knew that their source lay, not in any hostile feeling or purpose of the German people toward us (who were, no doubt as ignorant of them as we ourselves were), but only in the selfish designs of a government that did what it pleased and told its people nothing.

But they have played their part in serving to convince us at last that that government entertains no real friendship for us and means to act against our peace and security at its convenience. That it means to stir up enemies against us at our very doors the intercepted note to the German Minister at Mexico City is eloquent evidence.

We are accepting this challenge of hostile purpose because we know that in such a government, following such methods, we can never have a friend; and that in the presence of its organized power, always lying in wait to accomplish we know not what purpose, there can be no assured security for the democratic governments of the world.

We are now about to accept gauge of battle with this natural foe to liberty and shall, if necessary, spend the whole force of the nation to check and nullify its pretensions and its power. We are glad, now that we see the facts with no veil of false prtense about them, to fight thus for the ultimate peace of the world and for the liberation of its peoples, the German peoples included: for the rights of nations great, and small, and the privilege of men everywhere to choose their way of life and of obedience.

The world must be made safe for democracy. Its peace must be planted upon the tested foundations of political liberty. We have no selfish ends to serve.

We desire no conquest, no dominion. We seek no indemnities for ourselves, no material compensation for the sacrifices we shall freely make. We are but one of the champions of the rights of mankind. We shall be satisfied when those rrights have been made as secure as the faith and the freedom of nations can make them.

Just because we fight without rancour and without selfish object, seeking nothing for ourselves but what we shall wish to share with all free peoples, we shall, I feel confident, conduct our operations as belligerents without passion and ourselves observe with proud punctilio the principles of right and of fair play we profess to be fighting for.

I have said nothing of the governments allied with the imperial government of Germany because the yhave not made war upon us or challenged us to defend our right and our honor.

The Austro-Hungarian government has, indeed, avowed its unqualified indorsement and acceptance of the reckless and lawless submarine warfare adopted now without disguise by the imperial German government, and it has therefore not been possible for this government to receive Count Tarnowski, the Ambassador recently accredited ti this government by the imperial and royal government of Austria-Hungary, but that government has not actually engaged in warfare against citizens of the United States on the seas, and I take the liberty, for the present at

U. S. ARMED SHIP SUNK BY TORPEDO AT NIGHT; 11 DEAD, MANY MISSING

American Lieutenant and a Naval Guard in Charge of Aztec's Guns Believed Safe.

Paris, unofficially, Reports 19 Men Rescued, 29 Unaccounted for, While French Admiralty Message to Embassy Here States That Bluejackets and Captain, Together With Lieut. Fuller Graham, in Command of Gunners, Were Picked Up—Boat Upsets, Drowning 11.

Paris, April 2.—The American steamer Aztec has been sunk by a submarine near an island off Brest. Some of the crew were rescued and are being brought into Brest. A number of the men are missing and little hope is held that they can be saved, as the steamer was torpedoed at night while a heavy sea was running.

William Graves Sharp, the American Ambassador, was informed this afternoon by the French government of the torpedoing of the Aztec and immediately cabled the State Department.

Representatives of the American government will proceed to Brest to take the depositions of survivors of the disaster.

A French patrol picked up 19 of the crew of the Aztec. Twenty-eight men are reported missing.

Sixteen of Crew Americans.

New York, April 2.—The American steamship Aztec, owned by the Oriental Navigation Company, the first armed ship to sail from an American port, was sunk yesterday by a German submarine, according to advices received here tonight by the company from the United States consul at Brest, France.

The cable message gave no information as to the fate of the crew. There were 39 men aboard the vessel, 16 of them native Americans.

The Aztec sailed from New York March 18 [illegible]. She was commanded by Capt. Walter O'Brien.

The Oriental Navigation Company, owner of the Aztec, also owns the Orleans, one of the first American vessels to run successfully Germany's submarine blockade. The Aztec carried a full cargo of foodstuffs and general supplies valued at more than $500,000.

Carried Two 5-Inch Guns.

The Aztec was armed with two 5-inch guns, one forward and one aft. The crew of naval gunners on board was in command of a naval officer.

The Aztec, formerly owned by the Pacific Mail Steamship Company, was a ship of 3,727 tons gross and 2,345 tons net. She was built in Newcastle, England, in 1894. She was 350 feet long with a beam of 43 feet.

Americans in the Crew.

The following were the Americans among the crew and their addresses as filed here with the United States shipping commissioner:

I. J. Anderson, mate, Brooklyn, N. Y.; G. C. Larkin, second mate, West Lynn, Mass.; E. L. O'Brien, third mate, 60 Burgess place, Passaic, N. J.; B. Borjensen [illegible], Brooklyn, N. Y.; Harry Laskin, engineer, West Lynn, Mass.; Herbert Collins, engineer, 510 East Fifth street, Wilmington, Del.; Charles Erickson, engineer, Brooklyn, N. Y.; Chester T. Lee, steward, 111 Sacramento street, San Francisco; Henry T. Long, messman, New York city; Watson Saine, radio operator, New York city; Charles Kelly, Brooklyn, N. Y.; Julian R. Macomber, Honolulu; Charles Pineapolo, Honolulu; Ekela Keaka, Hawaii; Tato Davis, Hawaii, and H. K. Price, Hawaii.

Guard Believed Safe.

French admiralty dispatches to the French embassy here last night announcing the sinking without warning of the armed American merchantman the freighter Aztec, by a German submarine, and apparently Lieut. Fuller Graham and twelve American bluejackets, constituting the armed guard of the vessel, had been saved, but that eleven of the crew were reported missing.

The admiralty report said the Aztec, bound from New York to Havre, was torpedoed without warning Sunday off Ouessant. The torpedo struck squarely amidships, emitting a powerful gas and putting the wireless out of commission.

Guard in Second Boat.

The guard, with the captain and three other members of the crew in the second boat to put off apparently were picked up by the French patrol boat Sirrius after three hours. Eleven men are thought to hafve been drowned when the first boat to put off was smashed.

The third boat, containing the second officer and eighteen men is not directly accounted for, but the fact that only eleven are reported missing leads to the belief that it must have been picked up.

Will Not Stop Arming.

Officials said the disaster would not affect the policy of arming ships, which will be continued in the most efficient manner possible.

Secretary Daniels declined to make public the list of naval officers and gunners who manned the guns fore and aft on the Aztec.

"Until the survivors are listed and the department is officially advised concerning those whose lives may be lost," he said, "it will not announce the naval personnel of the Aztec."

ADRIATIC SAFE IN PORT.

Reaches England With Members of Harvard Unit Bound for France.

New York, April 2.—The steamship Adriatic, White Star Line, arrived safely at a British port last night, according to cable advices received here today.

She left here March 17 with 65 passengers, of whom 6 were American citizens. The Americans are members of a Harvard surgical unit on their way to France.

A former German passenger steamship, the Buelow, of 5,965 tons gross, arrived here today under the name of Tras-Os-Montes, and will be placed in trade between the United States and Bermuda, under charter by the Portuguese government to the Quebec Steamship Company. The vessel was self-detained at Lisbon when the war started, and was seized by Portugal wnen hostilities began between that country and Germany.

SPY BILL BEFORE HOUSE

Webb Measure Includes All Such Legislation Sought.

UNIVERSAL TRAINING IS ASKED

Kahn Would Call Young Men Between 18 and 22 to the Colors. Howard Introduces Act for Sale of Postal Savings Bonds to Raise Funds—Sundry Civil and General Deficiency Bills Also Introduced.

A comprehensive administration measure dealing with neutrality violations, espionage, injury to vessels, punishment for interference with foreign relations and commerce, falsification of passports, and other similar questions, was introduced yesterday by Representative Webb, of North Carolina, who will be chairman of the judiciary committee.

The bill embodies all the administration measures on those subjects which passed the Senate in the last Congress.

War Measures Predominate.

National defense, war measures, and bills for patriotic purposes predominated in the great number of bills introduced yesterday.

One of the first was by Representative Kahn, of California, to provide for universal military training for men between 18 and 22.

A resolution asking the President to designate June 14, the 140th anniversary of the birth of the American flag, as a day for the holding of patriotic meetings throughout the country, was introduced by Representative Siegel, of New York.

Proposes Postal Bond Sales.

A bill proposing the sale of postal savings bonds in small denominations from $1 to $100, introduced by Representative Howard, of Georgia, is designed to enable patriotic men and women to help finance the government. He predicted its enactment as a preparedness measure would result in raising at least $750,000,000 in 30 days.

The sundry civil and general deficiency appropriation bills were introduced. They are two of the supply bills that failed in the last Congress.

Would Congratulate Russia.

A concurrent resolution to congratulate the people of Russia on the establishment of a popular government was introduced by Representative Goodwin, of Arkaknsas, and referred without action to the foreign affairs committee.

*While the war with Germany was popular,
there were many that took exception to the
proposed draft system. Here and there
across the country, like this scene in
Rutgers Square on New York's lower East Side,
crowds gathered in anti-draft rallies.*

mered *ad nauseam* upon the theme in cartoon and type, created adverse publicity from which Daniels had never entirely recovered.

The two men were quite unlike. Baker was able to sell himself to his pernickety Regulars, but Daniels could never overcome the Navy's prejudices. Navy circles held that his timidity had obstructed naval preparedness. However, Daniels had a certain amount of common sense and also—to the nation's benefit, some people felt—he had a lively young assistant secretary named Franklin Delano Roosevelt.

In any event, the Navy's *enfant terrible*, Rear Admiral William Sowden Sims, the man who had shoved down the Navy's throat the necessity that naval guns shoot straight and sure, was on his way overseas by Daniels' order, to confer with the British Admiralty on the submarine situation and the necessity for convoys.

Truculent, spike-bearded Sims had stepped on many toes and would

*Throughout the nation, the people rallied
to the President and the war cause.
Pacifism was a dead issue.
In New York, the well-known woman artist
Neysa McMeinwell led patriotic parades.*

*Ex-President Theodore Roosevelt had long agitated for a chance to fight
in France at the head of a specially trained "elite" division.
But his repeated demands for action fell on deaf ears at the White House.*

step on many more. Seven years ago, the then Commander Sims had
disturbed both the German government and President William Howard
Taft himself when he told his listeners at a London banquet that,
should the British Empire be menaced by an external enemy, she could
count on "every man, every drop of blood, every ship and every dollar
of your kindred across the seas." Sims had earned a reprimand for that.
But that was 1910 and this was 1917; Daniels' choice of the peppery
sailor had Mr. Wilson's blessing.

The Navy Department's pressing task now was to get more ships,
both big and little. The "Great White Fleet" of Teddy Roosevelt's day
was in fact obsolescent, while there was a crying need for lighter craft
—destroyers and the like to hunt U-boats and convoy merchantmen.
So shipyards were already straining on a crash program. And the morning's mail was bringing the first of what would become a torrent of
offers from patriotic yachtsmen, from motorboat owners to millionaire
skippers whose oceangoing craft flew the swank burgee of the New
York Yacht Club—James Gordon Bennett's *Lysistrata,* J. Pierpont
Morgan's *Corsair,* and young Vincent Astor's *Nourmahal.* What would
soon be christened the "Splinter Fleet"—for coastwise anti-submarine
defense—was in the making.

Interesting things were happening elsewhere, too, this day. In New York, commuters on North River ferryboats saw a sleek four-piper destroyer slice quietly up-river to Hoboken, where the self-interned ships of the Hamburg-American and North German Lloyd lines, including the giant *Vaterland,* eased gently against their moorings. And there the destroyer, engines barely turning over against the tide, lay the rest of the day, like a wary barracuda, opposite the cluster of seemingly deserted liners.

And, as the morning papers explained in detail, a force of 12,000 New York metropolitan police had been mobilized and detailed to

With freedom's torch replaced by the shining sword of "Liberty,"
a familiar statue presented a new face for the world to see.

A NEW LIGHT

secure bridges, railroad yards and other sensitive points against possible sabotage. Units of the National Guard were already patrolling the reservoirs upstate. The Washington *Post* told of the incarceration in the Portsmouth Navy Yard of two residents of South Berwick, Maine, allegedly of German origin, who had been so indiscreet as to stretch a radio antenna from their barn to a tree.

Over in Paris, American flags blossomed over the Chamber of Deputies in the Quai d'Orsay, on the Senate building near the Luxembourg, and along the boulevards. From an equally bedecked London, a grave-faced American mining engineer—a Quaker named Herbert Clark Hoover—who had been doing a wonderful job of handling Belgian relief operations and whose neckwear resembled an Arrow Collar ad, cabled congratulations to President Wilson. And in Vienna, a young Second Secretary in the U.S. Embassy struggled with cabled instructions from home urging the ambassador to keep peace between the U.S. and the Austro-Hungarian Empire. His name was Allen Dulles.

Meanwhile, back in Washington, the President, after hearing of the Senate impasse, once again had relieved the tension of suspense by going out on the golf course. So he was absent that afternoon when Mr. Roosevelt arrived in town and dropped by the White House to express his pleasure with the war message. T. R. left a card and rushed on to his Oyster Bay home. If he couldn't reach the President in person with his military divisional dream, he would waste no time arguing with underlings at the War Department.

La Follette, the man who single-handedly had stymied the efforts of a President and a Congressional majority, spent the remainder of the day in strategy conferences with his pacifist friends. There was no doubt that the recalcitrant Republican meant business. His might be the last stand for the pacifist cause, but it would be as long and hard a stand as he could make it. He claimed to have heard from some 25,000 people, all endorsing his peace policy. And in the Senate he still had half of his original "group of willful men"—Stone of Missouri, Norris of Nebraska, Gronna of North Dakota, Lane of Oregon and Vardaman of Mississippi. The others had hauled down their flag of dissidence.

That night the President and Mrs. Wilson were cheered lustily as they attended the Belasco Theater. But in a crowded Washington restaurant Senator Vardaman was hissed out of the room when he refused to stand up for the "Star-Spangled Banner."

In the Senate, James K. Vardaman of Mississippi led the upper house opposition to America's entry into the war. Together with Senators Robert M. La Follette of Wisconsin, Asle J. Gronna of North Dakota, Harry Lane of Oregon, George W. Norris of Nebraska and William J. Stone of Missouri, Vardaman struggled to thwart the war resolution.

THE THIRD DAY

Eighty-two to Six

WEATHER
To-day. To-morrow unsettled. mild temperatures, with genial variable winds becoming fresh from the east.
Full Report on Page 14

New York Tribune

First to Last — the Truth: News · Editorials · Advertisements

CIRCULATION
Over 100,000 Daily
Net Paid, Non-Returnable

LXXVI No. 25,707   (Copyright 1917)
The Tribune Ass'n.]

WEDNESDAY, APRIL 4, 1917   • • •   ONE CENT In New York City

...nans Plot ...o Uprising ...he South

Prepare for Possible Rebellion When War Comes

...uton Schools of Propaganda

Agents Tempt the ...with Offers of ...ial Equality

(Correspondent of The Tribune)

... N. C., April 3. As in South Africa and India, a South secret agents of the German government have begun a revolt under the preaching Kultur. They have already working to bring of the negroes against ...

THERE CAN BE NO HEALING OF THE WOUND TILL THE THORN IS REMOVED

IMPERIALISTIC RULE OF MIGHT

Army to Pick Men in Drafts of 500,000

"Selective Conscription" to Raise Vast Force to Fight Germany

Daniels Planning Fleet Co-operation

President and Cabinet and Defence Council Hold Conferences

Washington, April 3. War aims, military, economic and financial, for aggressive hostilities against Germany only await action by Congress on a war resolution.

Action to-day was prevented by Senator La Follette. It is expected not later than Thursday.

President Wilson and his Cabinet went over the war plans at a two-hour session. Previously the National defence council, with its civilian advisory commission and several subsidiary organizations, developed policies and details.

The navy has taken steps to insure co-operation between the American fleet and those of the Entente Allies, to become effective upon the formal entry of the United States into the war.

Berlin Ignores U. S. Action; Will Refuse to Accept War; Backs Austria's Peace Move

Congress to Take Action On War Measure To-day

Senate Will Sit in Continuous Session to Wear Out Pacifists; La Follette Blocks Vote for a Day; House Ready to Back Wilson

[From The Tribune Bureau]
Washington, April 3. The Republican leaders, who conferred to-day, decided that as far as the minority was concerned the special war session might adjourn within three weeks. This may seem over-optimistic, but it is entirely possible.

Proposes Still to Treat This Country as Any Other Neutral

Thought of a Peace Conference Is Urged

Czernin's Overture Is Sanctioned by Germany and All of Her Allies

Berlin, April 3. The press report of President Wilson's "state of war" message reached Berlin at 10 o'clock this morning. It is declared here that there will be no change in the German attitude, even if Congress adopts President Wilson's view.

Germany will not declare war on the United States as it has been conducting since February 1, but this, the officials declare, in not directed more against the United States than any other neutral.

Central Empires Sanction Czernin's Plans for Peace

Will Be Approved at Conference of Rulers, Says Berlin Newspaper

London, April 3. The semi-official Berlin "Lokal Anzeiger" declares the proposal of the Austro-Hungarian Foreign Minister that a peace conference be held by the belligerents was sanctioned by all the Central Allies, and will be formally approved by a conference of high personages from the Dual Monarchy.

Phantasy of U. S. Troops Abroad

By C. W. Gilbert

WASHINGTON, April 3. In the enrollment of these days all sorts of nonsensical ideas are current about raising and sending large armies to Europe to fight against Germany. An army of a million men in the trenches in the favorite suggestion, though the numbers run sometimes as high as 3,000,000 to 5,000,000 men...

United States Co-operating with Allies; Cabinet Plans Naval Moves

By STEVENSON H. EVANS

Washington, April 3. The Republican leaders, who conferred to-day, decided that as far as the minority was concerned...

State Department, Other U. S. Offices Invaded by Spies

Washington, April 3. The "significance of President Wilson's warning of German spies..."

Curfew for M. O. Tricksters

Out from the office of the Self-Help Leagues into the homes of the poor go the inviting offers of little work for big money.

The Widow Jones sends the $2 asked to cover cost of "material."

Thereafter there's activity in Washington at the Solicitor's office of the Postoffice Department. Samuel Hopkins Adams describes the work of the Protector of the Poor in a fact filled article in next Sunday's Tribune.

A word to your newsdealer today will protect your copy.
You will not forget this story.

The Sunday Tribune

Capital Would Oppose Blind Peace Conference

Washington, April 3. Reports from official circles here...

THE THIRD DAY

Eighty-two to Six

THIS APRIL 4—Spy Wednesday in the liturgical calendar—dawned sunny and cool across a United States beginning to feel the grip of war hysteria. It had not yet, of course, erupted into the window-breaking, stone-throwing, arsonist stage, but roughhousing of pacifist meetings had become old hat. And already people whose only sin was speaking English with a Teutonic accent were beginning to feel it, in the averted glance of a neighbor, the undeclared boycott and the poison tongue of gossip. A few butchershops, their enterprising proprietors seeking patriotic pennies, were replacing the old "hamburger" signs with "liberty steak" labels.

The hysteria spread even to the baseball diamond. During an exhibition game at Wichita Falls, Texas, between the Detroit Tigers and the New York Giants, Ty Cobb, sliding spikes high into second, not only severely slashed Charles Lincoln (Buck) Herzog, but then leaped on the sprawling second baseman with both fists, screaming "German!" The incident became the sports-page highlight of the week, for Cobb, sulking, then refused to play again against the Giants.

All across the country the rumor mills were clacking now, and Uncle Sam, like the proverbial old maid, was peeking under the bed for the German agents who might be lurking there. New Yorkers read in the *Tribune* a fantastic piece from Greensboro, North Carolina, alleging a vast but shadowy Negro uprising to be pending in the South, brought about by German agents and German gold. The front-page story hinted that the Ku Klux Klan might ride again as a patriotic riposte—perhaps a not unnatural embellishment at a time when D. W. Griffith's film *The Birth of a Nation* was still a subject of violent controversy.

The Emporia *Gazette* warned of a coming censorship, voluntary instead of compulsory. But, it assured its readers, this would be for the common good; it would curtain our military movements. The Washington *Post* quoted "a high Latin American authority" who foretold

Anti-German feeling reached into the baseball diamond when
Ty Cobb, the testy Detroit Tiger, purposely spiked New York Giant
infielder Buck Herzog while sliding into second base.
In the melee that ensued, Cobb fought Herzog because he was " a German."

112 / THE THIRD DAY

*Repeated acts of sabotage and the dread fear of
subversion from within prompted the not-so-subtle
admonition from the Brooklyn* Daily Eagle *to "Strike First."*

(an old story, now) a German invasion via Mexico, with a simultaneous
German military advance southeast into British Honduras. German
agents were alleged to have attacked a Russian diplomat, one Michael
Borzatovsky, who had been found in his Baltimore Country Club
bedroom seriously wounded by a pistol bullet. In Philadelphia, five
hundred special police had been sworn in to guard the municipal reservoirs, and under Ben Franklin's statue over the City Hall an unidentified elderly woman had rushed into a Navy recruiting station, screamed,
"Peace, peace, you are murderers!" and left as rapidly as she had come.

In Detroit, where Henry Ford had made the automobile business a
national industry and revolutionized the American way of life (he
would put on the road this year a cool half-million Model T's) men

In 1915, Henry Ford (above center) chartered the Scandinavian-
American Liner, Oscar II, to take "An expeditionary force
for peace" to Europe to "get the boys out of the trenches by
Christmas." The famed Peace Ship, skippered by Captain Hemmel,
seen raising his hat, was launched on a sea of journalistic
ridicule and the effort failed. Ford and his anti-war
friends were rebuffed by European leaders. By 1917, however,
with half-a-million Model T's on the road (the one at right
is typical), Ford had made an about face in his war views
and had wired President Wilson he was prepared to build
1,000 submarines and 3,000 motors a year at no cost to the government.

were working under patriotic impulse. For Ford, angel of the "Peace Ship" and of other anti-war causes, had turned off the tap; his money fountain wquld no longer gush for pacifist purposes. Ford was ready, he had wired the President, "to build 1,000 small submarines a year and 3,000 motors a year," if needed, and this without cost to the government.

To Pittsburgh's roaring complex of steel mills government contracts were already seeping, with promise of more to come; U.S. Steel announced that wage increases would begin next month. In his Skibo Castle in Scotland, Andrew Carnegie, father of the steel industry, nodded approval, his ten-million-dollar grant to the cause of international peace forgotten since 1914. The War Department announced that it planned to call for two million men if and when conscription became law.

Former President Taft, returning from a tour of the South on behalf of the League to Enforce Peace—an organization devoted to postwar adjustment in Europe— had just announced that "both the South and

the Southwest are ready for the conflict.... This part of the nation, some of which was deeded to Mexico by [Germany's] Foreign Secretary Zimmermann, has not an ounce of anti-war spirit...."

But Taft's view was directly challenged by Representative Claude Kitchin of North Carolina, who declared that the people of his state were opposed to war in overwhelming majority.

Small wonder that for the countless thousands riding the trolley cars all over the nation, for the commuters in the El trains circling Chicago's Loop and serpentining their way above New York City streets, for the other thousands who jammed the still newfangled subway in Manhattan, and for those who clung to the cable cars careening down San

A new mood suffused the nation.
Its pride in itself was no longer to be contained.

Long a staunch advocate of peace, Andrew Carnegie (left)
father of the nation's steel industries, seen here strolling
in New York with Lord Weardale, another pacifist,
sadly supported the Allied cause. As his steel mills boomed, he sat
in his Skibo, Scotland mansion and unhappily observed,
"All my air castles of world peace have fallen about me like a deck of cards."

Majority leader Claude Kitchin of North Carolina surprised
the House of Representatives when he announced he intended to vote
against the war resolution. He tried to rally anti-war
support but was overwhelmed. The house voted 737 to 50 for war.

Francisco's hills, there was but one topic: How soon would the Congress get around to declaring war on Germany?

The question was uppermost, this morning, in the minds of two totally dissimilar persons, widely separated in space. In Lincoln, Nebraska, William Jennings Bryan, at his desk in the office of his pacifist weekly *The Commoner,* was preparing, of all things, a message to Mr. Wilson offering his services as a private in the Army. And overseas, riding in the Madrid-Paris express, Major William Mitchell, of the Aviation Section of the U.S. Signal Corps, under orders to the French Army as an official observer, was already convinced that a combat air service was essential for victory in modern war.

Two newspaper men on opposite sides of the continent decided to do something about getting into uniform: lanky Harold W. Ross, of the San Francisco *Call,* and pudgy Alexander Woollcott, drama critic of the New York *Times.*

Reporters needling both Theodore Roosevelt and the War Department on the status of T.R.'s dream division struck pay dirt. Mr. Baker authorized the diplomatic announcement that the Department lacked authority under existing law to carry out the Colonel's pet project. But the hero of San Juan Hill would not concede. Slapping crop to his booted leg as the newsmen met him coming from a ride at Oyster Bay, Mr. Roosevelt reiterated that as yet he had "heard nothing . . . not a single thing" from Washington.

And in the golden-domed *World* building on Park Row, New York's "newspaper row," Herbert Bayard Swope, just back from Europe, was readying himself for another war-correspondence stint, this time under the American flag.

Just what sort of war was this to be? Swope, like the other few American newsmen who had been able to get a glimpse of the Western front, had some idea. The man in the street, however, despite the proposed increase in the armed forces, believed that at most only a "token" would ever go overseas if war came.

As war fever gripped the nation, William Jennings Bryan, the "Great Commoner," and one of America's leading and most vociferous pacifists, prepared to wire President Wilson from his Lincoln, Nebraska office offering his services as an enlisted man in the Army.

*Thin, irascible Harold W. Ross was a young reporter
on the San Francisco* Call *when war was declared.
He promptly quit his job, joined the army and
was shipped as a private to France.
After the war, Ross returned to New York
where he ultimately founded the* New Yorker *magazine.*

As veteran war correspondent Frederick Palmer put it, on his return from Europe at the end of 1916, "even the strongest advocate for a large army never breathed a word suggesting that a single soldier should ever be sent to Europe."

And this was the still prevailing situation. Readers of the New York *Tribune* learned from its front page, side by side with a detailed breakdown of the War and Navy Departments' proposed expansions, that the idea the nation would send large armies overseas was "nonsensical." To put even a million men abroad "is an utter impossibility," glibly wrote Washington correspondent C. W. Gilbert. He quoted alleged statistics to prove that to transport and supply American troops abroad in any great strength would mean "that England and France would starve." All this, however, was byplay.

On Capitol Hill in Washington the big show was about to open. The prologue came at ten o'clock in the morning, in the House of Representatives, where Virginia's Flood, chairman of the Foreign Affairs Committee, presented a joint resolution tailored to concur with the Senate's (both differed only in minor semantics from the document drawn by Flood the previous night). Desultory bickering was followed by a remanding of the subject until the morrow, and all eyes and ears now focused on the Senate chamber.

There Hitchcock of Nebraska once again formally presented the war resolution. His words sank in:

"I have been bitterly opposed to war... [but now] I cannot vote against war without doing a vain and foolish thing. It would only serve to weaken my country... when war is inevitable."

Claude A. Swanson of Virginia, citing the Zimmermann note as reaching "the lowest depths of national turpitude," stressed that "the issue is not peace or war; war has already been declared upon us."

Henry Cabot Lodge pulled out all the patriotic stops. "We have submitted to wrongs and outrages... with a long patience.... Both Democrats and Republicans must forget party in the presence of the common danger."

Upon the floor now rose Vardaman of Mississippi to lead the opposition. He hedged a bit, although at the same time crying havoc on those who desired war. Vardaman had several times previously stressed his patriotic background—a grandfather in the War of 1812, a father who "gave the best years of his life to the Southern Confederacy," and his own year of service in the Spanish-American War. He had been ruffled by the restaurant episode of the previous night, and he showed his irritation now when his opening words were followed by a visible and somewhat noisy exit from the gallery of a number of visitors.

"I don't care whether or not these people stay to hear me," he thundered. "...Men have lost their bearings and their poise.... Self-assumed superiority of mind, intolerance and bigotry, are attributes of little minds...." The German provocation had been great, he admitted. "But each Senator should remember that he may...be signing the death warrant of hundreds of thousands....I cannot believe that war is for the welfare of the world or the people of this nation." But there was nothing new in what he said, nor was it to the taste of this audience. So Vardaman resumed his seat without applause.

Stone of Missouri, following—he who had cast the one dissenting vote in committee yesterday—was careful to stress that while he would vote against the resolution, "If we declare for war there must be no halting. We know what war means, but when war is declared, honor and patriotism will demand that we shrink not from the mouth of hell. If Congress unfurls the battle flag...I shall at once stand in obedient salute...."

Then Norris of Nebraska took up the cudgels. He was bitter and uncompromising. "We," cried Norris, "are going into war upon the command of gold...war madness has taken possession of the financial and political powers of our country....I would like to say to this war god, You shall not coin into gold the lifeblood of my brethren...put the dollar sign upon the American flag!"

And that brought battling James A. Reed of Missouri bounding from his seat. "If that be not giving aid and comfort to the enemy," he cried, "...then I do not know what would bring comfort to...a Hapsburg or a Hohenzollern." His charge brought a flutter of applause. Norris subsided. The clock ticked along, and the arguments continued; somewhat boring now, for the speeches were repetitiously for war. And then the great white knight of the pacifist cause, Bob La Follette, came galloping into the lists with visor down and lance couched.

La Follette knew, of course, that he was speaking for a lost cause; that most of the anti-war opposition was peeling away. But La Follette needed no spur, no applause to bolster his assault. For more than three hours—some accounts say four—while darkness came and the lights went on, he ran the gamut of anti-war, pro-German propaganda appeal. He assailed the President's acts, he defended his own previous utterances. He had been "scurrilously libeled," he declared, because of his filibuster on the armed merchantmen debate. He reiterated his previous boast that more than 20,000 responses from his listeners approved of his attitude by a ratio of twenty to one.

By now some of the original visitors in the galleries had gone home to their suppers, but their places were immediately filled by others—not a few in evening clothes—and the waiting line outside was still

Drama critic of the New York Times, *Alexander Woollcott, a pudgy curmudgeon even in his youth, heeded his country's call, enlisted in the Army and went overseas. There he met another private, Harold W. Ross, and together, in a Paris print shop, they worked on a soldier's weekly newspaper,* The Stars and Stripes.

Herbert Bayard Swope, noted correspondent of the
New York World and first Pulitzer Prize winner,
prepared to depart once more for Europe,
this time as an American war correspondent with the A.E.F.

long. Around the rail encircling the Senate floor members of the House were clustered to listen to the great debate.

And then the man from Wisconsin really warmed up.

"We have wallowed in the mire at the feet of Great Britain.... We have been actively aiding her enemy in starving German women, children and old men... in principle Germany had the right to blindly destroy ships by submarines and mines... Germany is only doing what England is doing!"

When La Follette abruptly ceased, John Sharp Williams of Mississippi scornfully retorted that his speech would have "better become Herr von Bethmann-Hollweg than an American Senator.... I have heard from him a speech... pro-German, pro-Goth, pro-Vandal...." La Follette left the floor for the cloakroom as Administration supporters crowded the rostrum in monotonous rebuttal until, at 11:11 p.m. the thirteen-hour flood of oratory died and a vote was called.

One by one in alphabetical order, the eighty-eight Senators present answered to their names, in an emotionally muffled silence broken only by a murmur as each of six individuals answered "No!" Voting with the man from Wisconsin were fellow Republicans Asle J. Gronna of North Dakota and George W. Norris of Nebraska; and Democrats Harry Lane of Oregon, William J. Stone of Missouri, and James K. Vardaman of Mississippi—all of them "willful men" diehards.

The gavel banged on the Vice President's podium and the result was announced: eighty-two for, six against. And still silence lay on the assemblage, a pressure almost physical. It was as if, for the first time, Senators and audience alike realized that an irrevocable national step had been taken. Then the chamber adjourned. The third day had ended.

THE FOURTH DAY

Pillar of Fire

WEATHER
night and to-morrow. Moderate temperatures, with fresh east and southeast winds.
Full Report on Page 12

New York Tribune

First to Last — the Truth: News · Editorials · Advertisements

.CIRCULATION Over 100,000 Daily.
Net Paid. Non-Returnable

XXVI No. 25,708
(Copyright 1917)
The Tribune Ass'n

THURSDAY, APRIL 5, 1917

ONE CENT In New York City

Senate 82 to 6 for War; House To Act To-day

Stone, La Follette, Norris, Gronna, Lane and Vardaman the Six

Williams Arraigns Wisconsin Senator

Accuses Him of Exalting Germany Above America; Debate Covers 13 Hours

[From The Tribune Bureau]

Washington, April 4.—Late tonight, after thirteen hours' debate, the Senate, by a vote of 82 to 6, adopted this joint war resolution:

WHEREAS, the Imperial German Government has committed repeated acts of war against the government and the people of the United States of America; therefore, be it

RESOLVED, by the Senate and House of Representatives of the United States of America, in Congress assembled, that the state of war between the United States and the Imperial German Government, which has been thrust upon the United States is hereby formally declared; and that the President be, and is hereby authorized and directed to employ the entire naval and military forces of the United States and the resources of the government to carry on war against the Imperial German Government; and to bring the conflict to a successful termination all of the resources of the country are hereby pledged by the Congress of the United States.

At 10 o'clock to-morrow morning the House of Representatives will take it up. Before midnight to-morrow it probably will have been adopted by the House and sent to the President, whose signature will complete the formal act of going to war with Germany.

The six Senators who voted against the resolution were:

LA FOLLETTE, of Wisconsin.
GRONNA, of North Dakota.
NORRIS, of Nebraska.
STONE, of Missouri.
VARDAMAN, of Mississippi.
LANE, of Oregon.

The debate lasted thirteen hours, culminating in a three-hour address by Senator La Follette against the resolution, and exacting replies by Senator Williams, of Mississippi, and by Senator La Follette's own colleague from Wisconsin—Senator Husting.

La Follette Assails Wilson's Supporters Who Criticised Him

Senator La Follette began by reading a letter to Representative Helgesen, of North Dakota, from a North Dakota woman, protesting in behalf of her sex against the slaughter of men. The Wisconsin Senator was given close attention from both the floor and galleries. "I had supposed until recently," said La Follette, "that in the story of Senators and Representatives to vote to act their convictions on questions coming before them...

SOME ONE MUST VACATE

THERE ISN'T ROOM HERE FOR US BOTH!

London Seized With Hope of Sudden Peace

America Has Launched an Offensive Without Striking a Blow

Wilson Speech Changes Entire War Outlook

Germany Now Expected to Quit "Cold"—Austrian Ruler Eager for End

By ARTHUR S. DRAPER
[By cable to The Tribune]

London, April 4. Within the twenty-four hours following President Wilson's speech to Congress there has come a remarkable change of opinion regarding the length of the war. To-day I find a general belief that peace is but a matter of weeks.

There Were Speeches

By C. W. Gilbert

Washington, April 4.—For the first time in nearly a generation Congress is exercising its power to declare war. If the dreams of those who believe that this war is the war against war come true, it may be a long time before another occasion like this one arises.

Austria Prepares To Break Relations

Will Act as Soon as U. S. Declares War on Germany

Vienna, April 4 (via London, April 4).—It appears certain that Austria-Hungary will sever diplomatic relations with the United States if Congress declares that a state of war exists between America and Germany.

Central Powers Seek Peace, Is Report

London, April 4.—Reports received to-day from three sources indicate that a new peace offer will be made by the Central Powers.

Russian Attache Shot at Baltimore

Messenger from Petrograd Mysteriously Wounded Eight Days After Arrival

Baltimore, April 4. Michael Boratavsky, of the Russian Embassy in Washington, who arrived from Petrograd eight days ago with a document for the embassy from the Russian Minister of Finance, was shot while in the Baltimore Country Club early to-day. He is now in a hospital here.

Pacifists Start Nation-Wide Drive to Hamper U. S. in War

Defeated in their attempt to stop the war, the pacifists yesterday made a virulent attack on President Wilson.

Ruth Law Will Enlist in Aviation Corps

Ruth Law has yesterday from two months at the British and French flying fronts, is going to enlist when this country enters the war.

Government Acts To Eliminate Big Profits on War

One Plant Threatened with Seizure; Brass Industry to Sell at Cost

Washington, April 4. The government to-day invoked for the first time its drastic powers to affix an exorbitant war profits.

Wilson Speech Hits German Exchange

Berne, April 4. The effect of President Wilson's address to Congress on the German exchange rate can to send the mark down in 72 centimes, the lowest price on record.

Easter Music in the Churches

Easter Sunday in the New York churches is a splendid festival of song.

Besides the noted soloists who are members of choirs in the leading churches many musicians of the best orchestral societies and artists from the Metropolitan Opera House will sing.

On Saturday next The Tribune will publish the full musical programmes of over one hundred of the churches of greater New York. Make sure of this guide to good music by ordering Saturday's Tribune from your dealer to-day.

The Tribune

THE FOURTH DAY

Pillar of Fire

A GALE FROM THE NORTHEAST was making up along the Atlantic coast this Holy Thursday morning—April 5—and already the rain was reaching inland. In New York the Stock Exchange opened to a shaky start, but the blazoned headlines of the previous day's Senate action later brought an upward trend to trading in steel. The illusion of a bloodless war had reached the West Coast; readers of the Los Angeles *Times,* who might have felt some concern at yesterday's War Department statement of an impending draft call for two million men, learned in an editorial that "what the Allies need in Europe is not men but munitions"—a forecast that would have sent cold shivers up the backs of the Allied War Council and cheered the German Army General Staff no end.

Today, it seemed, was the day on which all suspense would cease. For the joint resolution declaring war against Germany would go to the House of Representatives for action. So agreed the newspapers, detailing in full the Senate's action of yesterday, and, in majority, editorially applauding the result.

In the Treasury Building in Washington, Secretary William G. McAdoo and his cohorts were putting the finishing touches on a budget totaling the unprecedented sum of $3,400,000. In Philadelphia, newspaper readers were regaled with a fe-fi-fo-fum rumor of a mass poison plot engineered by mythical German agents, as well as a rehash of the Southern Negro uprising canard.

In Cambridge, Massachusetts, the editor of the Harvard *Lampoon,* a gangling six-foot-six undergraduate of twenty-two years named Robert E. Sherwood, decided to throw up his job—and with it Harvard —to enlist.

Overseas, an agitated German government was pouring out spine-stiffening assertions that America's course could have no effect on the final outcome of the war. Also, though perhaps few, if any, American readers appreciated it, this morning there was an odd uncertainty in news emanating from the new Russian republic and the Eastern front.

Only twenty-one days had elapsed since the Czarist autocracy had been toppled—to the vast delectation of American public sentiment. But instead of the pure flame of a new and knoutless democracy rallying to victory against the Kaiser, as envisioned by so many unrealistic American intellectuals, so far only the rumbles of a vast indigestion were coming from the fumbling giant. American readers might take some comfort from the London-based rumors of a bed-ridden Kaiser, but an AP dispatch from Paris announcing the shelving of "Papa" Joffre, the portly hero of the first Battle of the Marne, was received with misgivings.

Speculative whispers on American national defense included the proposed ringing of Narragansett Bay—why only Narragansett Bay?—

Secretary of the Treasury William Gibbs McAdoo,
a strong war advocate, wanted to quit the cabinet,
raise a regiment and go to France. He remained, however,
in the President's cabinet and fashioned a financial scheme which
became a key factor in uniting the nation's morale and war effort—the Liberty Loans.

Opposing Foch, Pershing, Haig and the other allied commanders was the legendary Paul Von Hindenberg who with his alter ego, *Erich Ludendorff, guided the destiny of the German armies.*

against German invaders by use of steel nets. This mingled in the morning news with word that the Panama Canal terminals would henceforth close between sundown and sunrise.

In New York the trustees of the Church of the Messiah continued a five-day debate on what action should be taken to rebuke their pastor, the Rev. Dr. John Haynes Holmes, for his Palm Sunday sermon opposing war with Germany. Also in New York, a young man arraigned in Yorkville Police Court for calling Americans "a lot of skunks" during a pacifist rally at Madison Square Garden received a six-month workhouse sentence.

In Chicago an alleged wife-murderer by cyanide went free when a jury disagreed after thirty-six hours of deliberation. And up the Hudson in Sing Sing's "death row," Arthur Warren Waite, whose interest in impending war was something less than academic, received word of

SENATE MINORITY

STONE   LA FOLLETTE
WORKS   VARDAMAN
LANE   CUMMINS
GRONNA   NORRIS
CLAPP   JONES
KIRBY   O'GORMAN

*A harsh judgment on the dissenting few —
the small yet vocal band of isolationists are
relegated to the ignominy of an imaginary "Hall of Shame."*

chilling import. He would burn. The Court of Appeals had affirmed his conviction and sentence of murder in the first degree. The Waite case had attracted national attention. The New York dentist, by his own admission, had killed his father-in-law and tried to kill his mother-in-law. Object: a million-dollar estate that would come to his wife, whom he also planned then to kill. The defense gambit had been moral imbecility.

And in Washington a five-foot yellow-striped two-faced effigy—depicting on one side Stone and on the other Vardaman—dangled during the morning from a lamp-post at 14th and H Streets.

Three passenger liners had safely made the crossing to London despite the U-boats: the American Line's *St. Paul* and *Finland,* and the

White Star's *Cedric*. Both American ships carried naval guns and gun crews. But six other vessels, including one carrying 1,200 horses for the British Army and two carrying Belgian relief supplies, had been sunk. Most of their passengers and crews had been rescued. A radio message from Berlin to the German-owned Telefunken station at Sayville, L.I., proudly announced that in March U-boats had sunk 50,000 tons of Allied shipping. All this furnished the prologue to the session of the House of Representatives called for ten o'clock in the morning.

Oddly enough—was it numbness or simply oversleeping by late witnesses at the Senate debate of the day before?—neither the House floor nor the visitors' gallery were more than half full when Champ Clark

To Marechal Ferdinand Foch fell the honor of launching the final combined Allied offensives that were to bring the War to an end.

called the assembly to order and Flood of Virginia rose to deliver the resolution. Under the unanimous consent rule, a vote could be called after one hour of discussion, but for the moment the debate began without limitation.

Illinois Representative Fred A. Britten at once struck sparks when he challenged the sincerity of such members as might vote in the affirmative. Probably seventy-five per cent of the House, he declared, actually sincerely opposed entering the war.

"...There is something in the air—picking us up bodily and literally forcing us to vote for the declaration of war, when way down deep in our hearts we are as much opposed to it as our people back home."

Britten was right about the "something in the air" impelling the American people toward war, although he was wrong about the sentiments of "our people back home." True, in his own state, Chicago's 18th Ward was rocked by a civil war between two feuding Irish candidates for alderman. No one, it seemed, had time to worry about overseas war. So-called "wrecking crews," cars filled with rowdy, trigger-happy gunmen, roamed the streets, shooting up one another and battling police. In one fracas a police sergeant was badly beaten, and a Negro bystander was gunned to death.

But elsewhere in the Middle West, the anti-German ground swell was beginning to be felt, particularly in Wisconsin. Taut-chinned men of Teutonic extraction, whose fathers and grandfathers had fled Prussian tyranny to don Union blue in the Civil War, were remembering that they were Americans. Forgotten were the pacifist incidents of the past week—the threats to dynamite the buildings of the University of Wisconsin at Madison, which brought local National Guard troops to the rescue; the demand for a referendum actually inserted in local election ballots in Sheboygan; the rumpus in Milwaukee when the German-American Alliance urged voters to boycott all but pro-German candidates for the school board.

Nor had Congressman Britten, it seemed, paid attention to the announcement from the naturalization office in the Sub-Treasury Building in New York: Since March 1, 18,889 New Yorkers of German and Austro-Hungarian nationality had taken out first papers, while an additional 4,255 had become full-fledged American citizens.

The stir following Britten's remarks in the House had barely died down when he presented an amendment that would prohibit the landing of any U.S. force in Europe "until so directed by Congress."

Clarence B. Miller of Minnesota, fire-eating Republican, now flung a bucket of fat into the smoldering flames by reading what he declared to be an unpublished paragraph of the Zimmermann note:

Refusing to be swept up in the war hysteria, Rev. Dr. John Haynes Holmes of The Church of the Messiah in New York preached, "If war is right, then Christianity is wrong, false, a lie . . . Other clergymen may pray to God for victory of our arms, I will not." The church trustees took issue with their pastor and sought to rebuke him. And the nation's clergy agreed—with the trustees.

136 / THE FOURTH DAY

"Agreeably to the Mexican government, submarine bases will be established at Mexican ports, from which will be supplied arms, ammunition and supplies. All [German] reservists in the United States are ordered into Mexico. Arrange to attack all along the border."

Despite almost immediate denial from the State Department of the authenticity of Miller's allegation, he stuck to his story throughout the session.

Then Claude Kitchin, House majority leader, took the floor, to defy, he said, the criticism that would follow his vote against war.

"I know that...I shall not only be criticized but denounced from one end of this country to the other. The whole yelping pack of defamers and revilers...will at once be 'sicked' upon my heels." A ripple of applause, led by Senator La Follette, who was a spectator, followed his words. Kitchen then belligerently asked whether or not the United States, if placed in a situation similar to that of Germany, would not violate neutrality, and he answered his own question with a vehement "yes." But, as in yesterday's Senate debate the dissenters had hedged, so finally did Kitchin. Vitriolic as he was, he nevertheless concluded by pledging support to the government after war was declared. He subsided in a medley of applause and hisses.

James T. Heflin of Alabama hotly attacked Kitchin's stand. "Had I contemplated such action as that taken by the gentleman from North Carolina, the majority leader of the House, I would have made out my resignation as leader first, then made the speech, and then resigned from the House."

At that Heflin's fellow Alabamian John Lawson Burnett erupted, calling on Heflin to prove his own patriotism by enlisting as a private in the Army. The pair went into a low-comedy shouting match, providing the session with badly needed comic relief. It ended when the sergeant-at-arms, with uplifted mace of office, herded Burnett to his seat.

Perhaps the heaviest single jolt to the pacifists was delivered while the Emergency Peace Federation, from its New York office at 70 Fifth Avenue, was announcing that it would "fight to a finish" to obstruct American war measures. At that very moment Representative John J. Fitzgerald, a firebrand Fenian from Brooklyn to whom anything British was anathema, was on his feet, urging—to the astonishment of many—"cooperation in every way with the nations who are to be our allies."

Then rose Joseph Gurney Cannon of Illinois—"Uncle Joe" to all

Speaker of the House Champ Clark (left) once a bitter foe of
President Wilson, led the war resolution through seventeen hours
of debate. At 2:45 a.m., Good Friday morning, the first
roll call was taken. At 3:15 a.m., April 6, 1917, America was at war with Germany.

Joseph ("Uncle Joe") Gurney Cannon of Illinois, a veteran of the House
of Representatives for many years, wholeheartedly supported
the Declaration of War. However, when Jeanette Rankin was reluctant to vote,
he is reported to have told her, "You cannot afford not to vote.
I shall not advise you how to vote, but you should,
one way or the other, as your conscience dictates."

Americans—the 81-year-old cigar-chomping autocrat of the House, to nail his colors to the mast before a cheering audience.

"Great heavens, what a country we have and what resources to call upon in time of war!...men, wealth, resources greater than those of any other nation on earth.... We are not as well prepared for war as we should be—we must get ready.... I am one-fourth German, one-fourth French and one-fourth English, but I am an American."

His final words, each one emphasized by a fist pounding on the desk before him—"I - shall - vote - for - this - resolution!"—brought a rolling drumfire of applause.

The afternoon drifted on, the floor and the galleries now full, despite the pelting rain outside. Everyone, it seemed, wanted to get into the act. At seven o'clock in the evening Speaker Champ Clark announced, "We will stay in session till the early hours of the morning, and all night if necessary." By nine o'clock a suggestion that debate close at 11:45 was drowned in a roar of "No's!" So unlimited debate was ruled out and the five-minute limit substituted.

The President's time during this long day had been taken up with conferences with Treasury Secretary McAdoo, who was planning a financial measure that would in two weeks become the Liberty Loan Act, and with his pet scheme of uniting public opinion. As envisioned, the propaganda operation would be run by a committee consisting of the Secretaries of State, War and Navy. At the moment, among several names being considered by the active steersman of the scheme was that of a well-known Western newspaperman, George Creel.

During the day Mr. Wilson also found time to peruse some of the

Veteran newspaperman George Creel became the nation's propaganda chief and was named chairman of the Committee on Public Information.

more interesting items in the flood of mail and telegrams coming into the White House. Among these was a laconic wire from the world's heavyweight champion, Jess Willard: "I will fight."

Mr. Wilson was in bed long before the session in the House ended. For midnight came and went, and still the flood of oratory swept on. By half past one in the morning eighty speeches had been clocked. At 2:45 a.m., the last of more than one hundred speakers ceased; some seventeen hours of debate were ended. The Britten amendment was promptly rejected. Monotonously the roll was then called on the big question and monotonously answered, until the name of Rankin was reached. Miss Rankin, who had arrived on the floor just in time, kept silence. As the clerk resumed his call, "Uncle Joe" Cannon hurried over and whispered in her ear. When her name was reached again on the second call, the lady from Montana rose shakily to her feet and mumbled something to the effect that she loved her country but could not vote for war. Barely audible were her final words: "I vote No!" And then Jeanette Rankin burst into tears as she sank back in her chair.

It was shortly after three o'clock when the last vote was counted and the tally announced: For a declaration of war, 373; against, 50. Just time to make the last editions of the Eastern mornings and ensure full national coverage.

It was Good Friday morning.

One hundred and seventy-five miles to the north and east of Washington an enormous pillar of flame and smoke towered over the surf-frothed Atlantic coast, with a sixty-five-mile gale licking sheets of sparks inland. Four square blocks of Asbury Park's clustered but fortunately unoccupied wooden summer hotels and boardinghouses were burning, out of control, while firemen from a fifty-mile radius struggled to dynamite a fire-break and save the city, and New Jersey National Guard units assembled to prevent looting. A defective fuse worth ten cents had ignited a million-dollar bonfire to punctuate Uncle Sam's declaration of war.

As America girded itself for the struggle, world heavyweight champion Jess Willard telegraphed the President, "I will fight."

THE FIFTH DAY

To Fight the Kaiser

WEATHER
to-day. To-morrow prob-
air. Not much change in
erature. Southwest gales.
Full Report on Page 14

New York Tribune

First to Last — the Truth: News · Editorials · Advertisements

CIRCULATION
Over 100,000 Daily
Net Paid, Non-Returnable

XXVI No. 25,709   FRIDAY, APRIL 6, 1917   ONE CENT In New York City

NOW WHAT'LL IT BE, PLEASE?

---

anzista
ps Move
ward U.S.

Against Villa,
an Officials
Explain

Scouted
At Washington

Soldiers Cannot
ious Damage,
Heads Say

Associated Press

$1,000,000 Damage Caused by Fire At Asbury Park

Blocks of Hotels and Boarding Houses Are Destroyed

Asbury Park, N. J., April 6. Flames driven by a sixty-mile gale, had early this morning licked up almost four blocks of hotels and boarding houses a block from the ocean front...

All Petrograd in Vast, Silent Cortege Honors Heroic Dead

Mighty Procession, Carrying Those Who Fell in Revolution, Marches to Ringing of Church Bells—Prison Guns Boom Salute as Victims Are Buried

Petrograd, April 6. The victims of the revolution were solemnly buried to-day in the historic field of Mars...

Rasputin's Court Sponsor Is Sent to Prison

London, April 6.—Mme. Virubova, the lady-in-waiting who introduced Gregory Rasputin, the mystic monk, to the Russian court, has been brought from Tzar-koe-Selo to the Tauride Palace...

18,889 Teutons Get Their First Papers Before Last Day

No Subjects of an Enemy Country Can Be Naturalized After War, Says Schneider

Since the Kaiser put his pen into our restricted submarine frightfulness into effect 18,889 Germans, Austrians and Hungarians of New York have taken out first papers...

Officials Seize Four Interned German Ships

The first step toward taking over the eighty-seven German vessels now in American ports was taken by the Federal authorities yesterday...

War Summary

The war resolution was adopted by the House and will be from the Senate and will probably be signed by the President before noon to-day. Then the United States will be at war with Germany.

Yesterday the Executive Departments of the government called upon Congress for immediate war appropriations aggregating $3,500,000,000. That is $33 per capita for the whole nation.

The army alone calls for $2,-932,537,933. Plans are prepared for raising at once a civilian army of 1,000,000 men, to be increased within twelve months to 2,000,000.

On Page 4 will be found a full account of the mobilization of the country's potential resources.

An issue of $2,000,000,000 3½ per cent government bonds is imminent. War currency has already been printed. (Page 3.)

A Department of Munitions may be created by the government, with a seat in the Cabinet.

A Commercial Economy Board has been formed by the Council of National Defence to "mobilize" the country's industrial and agricultural waste...

The War Board at Washington has drafted a rigid news censorship bill.

Americans in Belgium May Face Internment

Von Bissing Ready to Act, Report Says

London, April 5. A dispatch to the Exchange Telegraph from The Hague says:

"A frontier correspondent asserts that he understands General von Bissing, the German Governor General in Belgium, intends to order the internment of all Americans between the ages of seventeen and forty-five living in Belgium..."

Navy, 197,000 Men; Million For the Army

Land Force to Include 500,-000 To Be Obtained by Draft

Bills to Carry Out Wilson's Plans Ready

Call to Go Out Immediately for 15,000 Naval Militia and Reserves

Washington, April 5.—The vast scope of the Administration's plans for a war army and navy was revealed to-day after a military budget of $3,500,000,000 had been submitted to Congress.

In broad terms, it is proposed to triple the combined strength of the navy and to have in active service a war army of a million trained men, including the first 500,000 to be brought to the colors by selective conscription.

Bills to carry out the programme already are in the hands of the Congressional Military and Naval committees.

The budget is divided so that $2,-932,000,000 goes to the army and $468,000,000 to the navy...

Wilson Approves Army Bill

The army bill, drafted by the General Staff, has been approved by President Wilson, and the department decided to-day to make it public immediately upon passage of the war resolution by the House...

America Discovers the World

Earnest, narrow and sure of itself was this America, with a continent all its own and the world well lost. It was a wistful vision, and I do not believe that the men who by their up-to-date knowledge and wide vision of their responsibilities...

War Staff Opposed Transfer of Wood

Military Redistricting Called a Blow to Defence

Washington, April 5. From trustworthy sources it was learned to-day that the transfer of the Department of the East and the transfer of General Wood were neither approved nor approved by the War College or the General Staff...

The Fraud Order Thunderbolt

When a fraud order finally hits a mail order scheme another source of easy money is shut off for good

But in spite of the efforts of the Postoffice Department there still are a number of crooked thinking gentry operating in the United States whose ingenious schemes deprive the poor and credulous of millions of dollars a year.

Samuel Hopkins Adams tells in next Sunday's Tribune of the methods of these Wallingfords and the Postoffice is acting to protect the public. In fiction, Adams makes the truth more interesting than fiction. See that your dealer saves your Sunday Tribune.

War With Germany to Begin To-day

The Passing America
By C. W. Gilbert

WASHINGTON, April 6.—Representatives are simpler people than Senators, nor the talk in the lower house was simpler and more immediate than the talk yesterday. You got what you didn't get in the Senate, a "close-up." I am driven to some metaphors of the vanishing America, the America of self-sufficing provinciality...

House Adopts Resolution After 3 A. M.; Debates 17 Hours

Vote 373 For And 50 Against

Kitchin Bolts and Leads Little Pacifist Band in All-Night Fight

Washington, April 6.—The resolution declaring that a state of war with Germany exists was adopted by the House shortly after 3 o'clock this morning by an overwhelming vote. All amendments had been rejected, and the resolution is in precisely the form in which it passed the Senate. The debate had lasted seventeen hours, and more than 100 members had taken part.

The vote was 373 to 50. The resolution will go to the President this morning, and he is expected to sign it before noon. Then this country will be formally at war.

Those voting against it were Miss Rankin; Almon, of Alabama; Bacon, Britten, Browne, Burnett, Church, Cary, of Wisconsin; Connelly, of Kansas; Cooper, fo Wisconsin; David: Davis, Decker, Hensler, of Miss-ouri; Hilliard, Colorado; Igoe, of Missouri; Johnson, of South Dakota; Keating, of Colorado; King, of Illinois; Kinkaid, of Nebraska; Kitchin, of North Carolina; Knutson, of Minnesota; La Follette, of Wisconsin; Little, of Kansas; London, of New York; Lundeen, of Minnesota...

Kitchin Leads Pacifists, Mann Joins War Party

Counteracting the influence of Kitchin, the Democratic floor leader, who led the fight against the declaration, was the influence of Republican Leader Mann and Representative Fitzgerald, of Brooklyn...

THE FIFTH DAY

To Fight the Kaiser

IN THE GRAY DAWN of this Good Friday—in 1917 a day of veneration for both Christian and Jew, for Passover would begin at nightfall—detachments of troops and bluejackets seized 104 German merchant-men lying in American ports. The biggest group was, of course, in New York harbor. It included the majority of twenty fine passenger liners familiar to the New York waterfront.

New York's Collector of the Port, Dudley Field Malone, backed by a detachment of the 22nd Infantry from Governors Island, took formal possession of the buff-stacked vessels at the Hoboken piers. Among them were such well-known ships as the monster *Vaterland* of the Hamburg-American Line and her lesser, but fat, comfortable sister *Amerika,* and the two *Presidents, Grant* and *Lincoln.* There, too, lay the crack four-piper flyers of the North German Lloyd—*Kaiser Wilhelm II*—and the *George Washington.* The *Kronprinz Wilhelm* was at Norfolk; the *Kronprinzessin Cecilie* at Boston.

Commodore Hans Ruser, commander of the *Vaterland* and senior officer aboard the German ships, met Malone at the foot of his gangway. The men were old acquaintances.

"We are ready," said the German, smiling sadly. And then, head erect, the skipper respected for years by thousands of American trans-atlantic travelers marched with his 1,214 officers and men to intern-ment on Ellis Island.

There was reason for the sadness in Ruser's smile; it was the grief of the sailor whose ship is wrecked. For, as Federal officials found when they went aboard, below decks each of the ships was the scene of a methodically contrived chaos; sabotage had been conducted with typical German thoroughness.

In each ship the main power plant had been the principal target. Engine cylinders—except for the turbine-driven *Vaterland,* all these ships were powered by reciprocal engines—had been crushed by hy-draulic jacks; holes gaped where broken sections had been pried away.

America's first act of war took place at dawn in Hoboken, New Jersey.
Backed by a detachment of the 22nd Infantry, Port of New York Collector
Dudley Field Malone formally seized the crack Hamburg-American liner, Vaterland,
and marched the crew off to internment. Though the huge German ship was
badly sabotaged, it was eventually repaired and sailed as the troopship Leviathan.

Warped and severed connecting rods told their tale of blowtorch application. Inside the *Vaterland's* turbine casings the delicate blades lay heaped in shards—sheered off by tools and metal bars dropped in while the engines were turning over.

Main shafts of engines deliberately run without oil had seized in their melted bearings. Water lines had been disconnected, ruptured or cunningly cross-coupled, electric communications torn out or shorted, auxiliary engines and pumps smashed by sledges. As a final touch, not a single manual or diagram remained in any engine room to aid restoration.

From a German viewpoint, it had been a splendid job. Off-the-cuff estimates by head-shaking naval experts indicated that it would take years of normal shipyard time to put any of these vessels in running order—time that could not be spared by American yards already running at capacity to replace U-boat casualties and also to handle the urgent demands of the U.S. Navy. And that, of course, was exactly what the German government had counted on when it had deliberately written off the pride of its merchant marine. If Germany couldn't have these ships, nobody would.

The weather was clearing in the Eastern area of the nation. The embers of Asbury Park's burned-out area were still smoldering. The Attorney General of the United States—Thomas W. Gregory—sent out agents of the Department of Justice on a grab hunt for sabotaging Germans—actually some 60 alleged ringleaders would be corralled—and announced that "no German alien enemy in this country who has not hitherto been implicated in plots against the interests of the United States need have any fear . . . so long as he observed the following warning: 'Obey the law and keep your mouth shut!'"

Months of anger, frustration and revulsion underlay this deeply
sarcastic comment on Germany's policy of unrestricted submarine warfare.

"Germany never had the slightest intention of attacking the United States of America, and does not have such intention now."

In Chicago a twenty-one-year-old girl who had gone driving with an unidentified man was found mysteriously murdered under a gloomy rear stairway of a South Side nightclub. In Washington striking employees of the Washington Railway and Electric Company were accused of dynamiting trolley poles on the right-of-way.

An anonymous giver sent an Iron Cross with an embossed picture of a bull in the center and four white feathers on each side to Senator La Follette. The emblem, postmarked Philadelphia, bore the inscription

Among the many gallant doughboys who served in France was a mild, bespectacled captain with the 129th Field Artillery. His name was Harry S. Truman.

*Anticipating final congressional approval later in the day
the Brooklyn* Daily Eagle *cartoon for April 6, 1917,
shows America already taking her place beside her new allies.*

"from William II." The University of Pennsylvania dismissed Professor
Simon N. Patten for having taken active part in a pacifist meeting two
days previously.

The press carried full coverage of the House debate, with pertinent
editorial comment. Even the Chicago *Tribune* stressed the necessity for
"an army of obligatory citizen service," which should be established
"permanently as the foundation of the nation's defenses." Readers of
William Allen White's Emporia *Gazette* were served religion-*cum*-
patriotism under the title: "A Holy Day." "America," editorially advised White, "is waging a war for the very brotherly love and good will
for which Christ went to his death on Good Friday." But James Cardi-
nal Gibbons in Baltimore contented himself—and his hearers—with the
admonition: "In the present emergency it behooves every American
citizen to do his duty, and to uphold the hands of the President and the
legislative department..."

When the news hit Kansas City, Missouri, a cocky thirty-three-year-

Ruth Law, an American aviatrix, was the only woman allowed
to wear a uniform for non-military purposes in France.
She toured French air bases and actually flew over the war-torn Western Front.

old former National Guardsman (two three-year hitches) who was trying to run his grandfather's farm near Grandview, and also nurse along an oil-well promotion company, foregathered with old comrades. Object, to recruit a new regiment of Missouri field artillery. His name was Harry S. Truman.

And in New York, the leaders of the Emergency Peace Federation of the Women's Peace Party and the American Union Against Militarism decided to abandon their projected joint campaign to support opposition to the war by providing free legal aid to militant objectors.

Ruth Law, American aviatrix, also in New York, reiterated her announcement, made after returning from a visit to French Army aviation camps, that she would "enlist as an instructor of American aviators." She had not, it seemed, received any answer from the U.S. Army to her initial offer.

All these things were, of course, prelude to the day's big event, the official finale. It was noon when Vice President Thomas R. Marshall in Washington, in his capacity as President of the Senate, signed the joint resolution declaring a state of war between the United States and Germany, then sent it posthaste to the White House.

The President and Mrs. Wilson, foregoing their usual daily golf game, had instead taken a brisk walk up Connecticut Avenue to Dupont Circle and back. On their return the President, smiling, politely doffed his hat to a group of suffragettes picketing the White House with banners reading, "Russia and England Are Enfranchising Women." An

A man of superior intelligence, inspiring eloquence and unshakable idealism, Woodrow Wilson was further blessed in his choice of his second wife, the former Edith Bolling Galt, whom he married in 1915 during his first term in office.

Across the country, the nation's press reported the growing tension as the long days of debate drew close to the hour of decision. Reproduced here (above) is the front page of the New Orleans Times Picayune for April 6, 1917.

The official Declaration of War, shown in the composite photo (Right), was signed by the President, using a borrowed pen, with only his wife and a cousin, Miss Helen Woodrow Bones, as witnesses.

instant later, a gust of wind jolted the Presidential dignity by lifting his topper, but a Secret Service man deftly retrieved it.

On the White House veranda they were met by Cousin Helen Bones, while at the door stood Mr. Wilson's assistant secretary, Rudolph Foster, and veteran chief usher "Ike" Hoover, the latter with the Congressional document in his hand.

The President took it, marched into the little "waiting" study and sat down, his wife and cousin standing beside him.

Here were no crowding newsmen, no background of officials jostling to get into the picture, no battery of souvenir pens. Actually, Mrs. Wilson had to find a pen and hand it to the President. Meanwhile Hoover, Foster and the naval aide, Lieutenant Commander Byron McCandless, stood outside the open door.

Mr. Wilson boldly scrawled his signature and handed the pen back to his wife. Foster ran to tell the White House correspondents and

McCandless dashed out on the drive, to face the State, War and Navy Building. His fluttering arms semaphored a prearranged signal to someone standing at a Navy Department window, and that was that.

The United States was at war with Imperial Germany. In Washington, where the sun was shining and the flags stood out stiff in the brisk breeze, the clock hands pointed to 1:18 p.m.; it was 12:18 in Chicago, 11:18 in Omaha, and only 10:18 in San Francisco. But overseas, night was falling; it was 6:18 in London and Paris, and an hour later in Berlin.

In Catholic churches around the nation, gaping tabernacle doors and purple-shrouded crucifixes and statues attested to the fact that this was still Good Friday. But the weather was clearing and Easter with its joyous parades was but two days away. So the strains of the "Star-Spangled Banner" rose that night from a thousand places, from flag-wrapped Geraldine Farrar on the stage of the Met to the humblest movie and honky-tonk.

America, as Americans had known it, would never again be the same.

EPILOGUE:

Never Again the Same

(Above) *President Wilson is blindfolded prior to drawing the first capsule in the draft lottery held under the Selective Service Act.*

(Below) *Among the first National Guard units mobilized as hostilities began was this unit in Chicago seen leaving for training camp.*

EPILOGUE:

Never Again the Same

MR. WILSON'S SIGNATURE on the declaration of war would start some two million Americans overseas to war. It would be a long road and a difficult road for those buoyant youngsters of a generation brought up in the Quixotic atmosphere of the slouch-hatted, open-throated Spanish-American War. They would march now in John J. Pershing's buttoned-up war.

They would cross the seas by grace of the U.S Navy and the convoy system devised by Admiral Sims; no U-boat would ever sink an eastbound troop transport. The way would begin in the wide sea-lane opening up in New York Bay, with the Statue of Liberty on the starboard hand and, a little farther along, Coney Island's huge gray wooden elephant to port. They would pause in a Breton mud-hole named Pontanazen, and then the road would take them through the grim recesses

One major obstacle to the rapid reinforcement of the Allied armies was the need for training in the type of warfare the men would have to wage. Trench hurdling was part of the course.

of the Argonne Forest, and they wouldn't stop until they reached Ehren-breitstein on the Rhine.

These men would be singing a song whose words, on this April 6, 1917, were still buried in the subconscious of a man named George M. Cohan:

"Over there, over there, we're going over,
And we won't come back till its over, over there."

They would go overseas on the crest of a technological and industrial wave unprecedented in proportion and undreamed of either here or abroad, for nobody had probed the depth of the country's potential resources, ingenuity and capability until they were put to the acid test. Many of these men would go abroad in the very ships that the Germans felt sure they had immobilized in American harbors.

For when the shipwrights shuddered at the extent of the damage, an

Propaganda posters, tacked to the walls of every post office throughout
the land, pictured our cause in Europe as a "holy crusade"
against an "infidel" Kaiser. On a more practical level,
they served to stimulate public interest in the purchase of Liberty Loan bonds.

(Above) *Swinging up Fifth Avenue,
the 69th Regiment marches
off to training camp.
Next stop: France and the bloody Western Front.*

HELP CRUSH *the*
MENACE *of the* **SEAS**

BUY LIBERTY BONDS
Buy Quickly   *Buy Freely*

RAINBOW DIVISION
SPECIAL
LIBERTY LOAN COMMITTEE

J.L.Grosse

**keep
these
off
the U.S.A**
Buy more LIBERTY BONDS

John Norton

For the war-weary allies, bled white by three years of slaughter,
the arrival of the first American troops in London was a tremendous boost
to war-weary morale. Their arrival rejuvenated the Allied will to fight.

No soldier of the A.E.F. who served in France would
ever forget the freight cars marked "Quarante Hommes—Huit Chevaux,"
better known as the "forty and eight," used for transport to and from the front.

American engineer named D. H. Wilson suggested to retired Commander A. B. Hoff that the almost miraculous properties of electric welding be invoked to repair it, and Hoff passed the word along. Within eight months the supposedly useless hulks would again be plying the Atlantic, this time under the American flag, and carrying, before the job was done, 558,000 American soldiers.

The men of the A.E.F. would exchange the rattling Els and the subways, and the plush comfort of Pullmans, for bumping, square-wheeled pigpens whose slatted sides were stenciled *"Quarante Hommes —Huit Chevaux."* Instead of kaleidoscopic glimpses of "Children Cry for Castoria" and whales being scrubbed white by Sapolio, they would blink at the blazoned praises of some weird product labeled *"Byrrh!"* but which wasn't beer at all. For the exhilarating pink-paged *Police Gazette* a more titillating substitute would be provided in *La Vie Parisienne*. The people back home might still be crooning "Sweet Adeline," but these soldiers and sailors would be roaring the far bawdier praises of "Mademoiselle from Armentieres."

Some of these men would find themselves in strange places indeed, and in circumstances they had never envisioned. Pfc. Alvin C. York

was caught in the draft and was finally convinced that a patriotic soldier could kill an enemy if necessary without endangering his soul. Pinned with his platoon of Company G, 328th Infantry, in the Argonne Forest, on October 8, 1918, under terrific enemy fire that knocked out nine men, including all three non-coms, York took over. Opening fire first with his rifle, then with his pistol, he shot down some fifteen German soldiers and stormed a machine-gun nest. Before he was through, the nest was taken and York, single-handedly, was corralling into captivity 132 Germans—4 officers and 128 men—and several guns, as his citation for the Congressional Medal of Honor would attest.

Only a few miles from the scene of York's exploit and four days later, Sam Woodfill, now wearing lieutenant's bars, circled a flank when his company was held up by machine-gun fire and killed four Germans, including an officer, in hand-to-hand combat. He cleared the obstruction, but they were held up again a few moments later by another machine-gun nest. So Woodfill led a charge against it, shooting or capturing its crew. Finally, alone, he charged a third machine-gun position, killed five men with his rifle and jumped into the pit, pistol in hand. Another machine gun opened up on him from one side. Woodfill missed the two-man crew with his pistol fire, so he grabbed a nearby pickaxe instead, and killed them both. Pershing called Woodfill "the bravest man in the U.S. Army." He, too, would wear the pale blue watered-silk, star-studded ribbon of the Medal of Honor for gallantry in action "above and beyond the call of duty." But, best of all, Sam had been able to marry his sweetheart before going overseas.

As for lawyer Charles Whittlesey, now a major, and known as "Galloping Charlie" to his men in the 3rd Battalion, 308th Infantry, he would earn fame and the Medal of Honor, too, by his leadership of the "Lost Battalion"—actually never "lost" but only surrounded—during five days of hell in the Argonne, not far from where York and Woodfill had accomplished their feats of derring-do.

Major Peyton March, leaving the General Staff to command the artillery of the First Division overseas, was shortly thereafter called back to Washington to become a full general and Chief of Staff, U.S. Army, and begin a lifelong feud with Pershing.

Flamboyant Major Douglas MacArthur, personally picked by Secretary Baker as chief of staff of the 42nd "Rainbow" Division, the National Guard's first unit to move overseas, was commanding it by the war's end—a brigadier general conspicuous in his troops' front lines for his immaculate uniform, outrageously nonregulation uniform cap, and above all for his daring. And Major Enoch Crowder as a major general, the Provost Marshal General, would administer the draft law he had brought into being.

Robert Sherwood of Harvard could not enlist in either the U.S. Army or the Navy, for recruiters threw up their hands at a six-foot-six toothpick frame on size seventeen shoes. So he went to Montreal and ended up overseas with Canada's kilted Black Watch—the "Ladies from Hell."

George C. Marshall served as
Pershing's operations officer with
the rank of Lieutenant Colonel.

Tragedy did not spare former
President Theodore Roosevelt.
His beloved youngest son, Quentin,
lost his life in aerial combat
over German lines in July 1918.

(Above) *Leading the vanguard of 1,750,000 doughboys to France,
Gen. John J. Pershing, A.E.F. commander, landed at Boulogne on June 13, 1917.*

(Below) *Nov. 11, 1918 was Armistice Day. The war with Germany ended.
This was the scene in New York City in front of the Public Library.*

He saw combat. But neither Harold Ross nor Alexander Woollcott ever went into battle. They would meet, instead, in a dingy Paris print-shop, with a joint mission: to help produce a zany, devil-may-care soldiers' weekly, the *Stars and Stripes*.

Herbert Bayard Swope of the *World* would get overseas as a correspondent with the A.E.F., on his brow the halo of the first Pulitzer Prize awarded for reporting, won for his previous coverage of the World War overseas.

And Captain Harry S. Truman on September 30, 1918 reached what at the time he must have considered the greatest day in his career. Acting as his own forward observer, he smashed a German counterattack near Exermont, in France, with the guns of his Battery D, 129th Field Artillery. This was during the last valiant fling of the over-eager, over-extended 35th Division.

General Leonard Wood, as he had feared, would never command troops overseas, for Presidents don't forget. Neither would Theodore Roosevelt, whose enmity against Wilson flared anew when his scheme of an elite division of his own was finally turned down. But his sons would go, and his youngest, Quentin, would die gallantly in action, fly-

The "war to end war" was over. In Paris, the Big Four met to write the terms of peace. Shown (left to right) *are Britain's Lloyd George, Italy's Vittorio Orlando, France's Georges Clemenceau and Woodrow Wilson.*

Names like Château-Thierry, Cantigny, Belleau Wood, St.-Mihiel
and Argonne would be added to the nation's battle streamers.
The war to make the world safe for democracy was a costly war.
In terms of dollars it came to $32 billion.
But, in grief, the cost was immeasurable. In all, 116,516 men
remain forever in the well-tended American cemeteries
in France such as this one at the site of the Argonne battlefield.

ing one of the combat planes that Brigadier General Billy Mitchell so earnestly craved.

Captain George C. Marshall, despite his initial misgivings, had gone overseas promptly to win a name for himself as an outstanding G-3 (plans and training officer), first in the "Big Red One," the 1st Division, and later at Pershing's own AEF headquarters. He was a temporary colonel, general staff, when hostilities ceased. Lieutenant Dwight D. Eisenhower was not so fortunate. The Armistice found him still in the United States, a temporary lieutenant colonel in the Tank Corps, training troops at Camp Colt, Gettysburg, Pa.

Grover Cleveland Bergdoll, Philadelphia playboy and latter-day "Man Without a Country," would successfully dodge the hot breath of conscription from August, 1917, to January, 1920, when the war was over. Then Federal agents, despite the threats of his pistol-brandishing mother, would drag him from a window-seat hideaway in the family home in Philadelphia to a military prison on Governors Island. Four months later, permitted to go home under guard to obtain documents allegedly of vital import to his appeal, he would slip through his captors' hands by a back door while trusting guards waited in front. This time his flight would carry him all the way to Germany. After nineteen years of oblivion, he would return voluntarily to do a four-year stretch in Leavenworth penitentiary for desertion in time of war, then fade into anonymity, "unwept, unhonored and unsung."

The men of the A.E.F. would come home after November 11, 1918 —except, of course, for the 115,000-odd who would never come back alive. They would come home to a changing nation, which they themselves would help to change further. For, as Tin Pan Alley, the barometer of our *mores,* quickly put it:

"How you gonna keep 'em down on the farm,
After they've seen Paree?"

And at Versailles Woodrow Wilson and the other victors would be busy with their shears, cutting up an old world and putting together a new one—an artificially contrived, shiny-varnished picture puzzle whose pieces, as it turned out, would never quite mesh. Allen Dulles would be a junior member of that delegation and would live to defend Wilson from a detractor in 1966.

But the greatest tragedy of all would be the deathblow that the Congress and the people would give to that stern idealist who, hating war, had led his nation into war to make a reality of his peace dream, the League of Nations. And not the least irony would be the fact that Mr. Wilson's former ally, war-hawk Henry Cabot Lodge, would join with pacifist Robert La Follette to keep the United States out of the League.

Yes, America would change. Its age of innocence had ended.

APPENDICES

A. German declaration of unrestricted submarine warfare

Washington, D.C., January 31, 1917

Mr. Secretary of State:

Your Excellency was good enough to transmit to the Imperial Government a copy of the message which the President of the United States of America addressed to the Senate on the 22nd inst. The Imperial Government has given it the earnest consideration which the President's statements deserve, inspired, as they are, by a deep sentiment of responsibility.

It is highly gratifying to the Imperial Government to ascertain that the main tendencies of this important statement correspond largely to the desires and principles professed by Germany. These principles especially include self-government and equality of rights for all nations. Germany would be sincerely glad if, in recognition of this principle, countries like Ireland and India, which do not enjoy the benefits of political independence, should now obtain their freedom.

The German people also repudiate all alliances which serve to force the countries into a competition for might and to involve them in a net of selfish intrigues. On the other hand, Germany will gladly cooperate in all efforts to prevent future wars.

The freedom of the seas, being a preliminary condition of the free existence of nations and the peaceful intercourse between them, as well as the open door for the commerce of all nations, has always formed part of the leading principles of Germany's political program. All the more the Imperial Government regrets that the attitude of her enemies, who are so entirely opposed to peace, makes it impossible for the world at present to bring about the realization of these lofty ideals.

Germany and her allies were ready to enter now into a discussion of peace, and had set down as basis the guarantee of existence, honor, and free development of their peoples. Their aims, as has been expressly stated in the note of December 12, 1916, were not directed toward the destruction or annihilation of their enemies and were, according to their conviction, perfectly compatible with the rights of the other nations. As to Belgium, for which such warm and cordial sympathy is felt in the United States, the Chancellor had declared only a

"Damn the Torpedoes! Go Ahead!"

few weeks previously that its annexation had never formed part of Germany's intentions. The peace to be signed with Belgium was to provide for such conditions in that country, with which Germany desires to maintain friendly neighborly relations, that Belgium should not be used again by Germany's enemies for the purpose of instigating continuous hostile intrigues. Such precautionary measures are all the more necessary, as Germany's enemies have repeatedly stated, not only in speeches delivered by their leading men, but also in the statutes of the Economical Conference in Paris, that it is their intention not to treat Germany as an equal, even after peace has been restored, but to continue their hostile attitude, and especially to wage a systematical economic war against her.

The attempt of the four allied powers to bring about peace has failed, owing to the lust of conquest of their enemies, who desired to dictate the conditions of peace. Under the pretense of following the principle of nationality, our enemies have disclosed their real aims in this way, *viz.*, to dismember and dishonor Germany, Austria-Hungary, Turkey and Bulgaria. To the wish of reconciliation they oppose the will of destruction. They desire a fight to the bitter end.

A new situation has thus been created which forces Germany to new decisions. Since two years and a half England is using her naval power for a criminal attempt to force Germany into submission by starvation. In brutal contempt of international law, the group of powers led by England not only curtail the legitimate trade of their opponents, but they also, by ruthless pressure, compel neutral countries either to altogether forego every trade not agreeable to the Entente Powers, or to limit it according to their arbitrary decrees.

The American Government knows the steps which have been taken to cause England and her allies to return to the rules of international law and to respect the freedom of the seas. The English Government, however, insists upon continuing its war of starvation, which does not at all affect the military power of its opponents, but compels women and children, the sick and the aged, to suffer for their country pains and privations which endanger the vitality of the nation. Thus British tyranny mercilessly increases the sufferings of the world, indifferent to the laws of humanity, indifferent to the protests of the neutrals whom they severely harm, indifferent even to the silent longing for peace among England's own allies. Each day of the terrible struggle causes new destruction, new sufferings. Each day shortening the war will, on both sides, preserve the lives of thousands of brave soldiers and be a benefit to mankind.

The Imperial Government could not justify before its own conscience, before the German people, and before history the neglect of any means destined to bring about the end of the war. Like the President of the United States, the Imperial Government had hoped to reach this goal by negotiations. Since the attempts to come to an understanding with the Entente Powers have been answered by the latter with the announcement of an intensified continuation of the war, the Imperial Government—in order to serve the welfare of mankind in a higher sense and not to wrong its own people—is now compelled to continue the fight for existence, again forced upon it, with the full employment of all the weapons which are at its disposal.

Sincerely trusting that the people and the Government of the United States will understand the motives for this decision and its necessity, the Imperial Government hopes that the United States may view the new situation from the lofty heights of impartiality, and assist, on their part, to prevent further misery and unavoidable sacrifice of human life.

Inclosing two memoranda regarding the details of the contemplated military measures at sea, I remain, etc.,

(Signed) Von Bernstorff

[Memoranda Inclosed in the Bernstorff Note]

From February 1, 1917, sea traffic will be stopped with every available weapon and without further notice in the following blockade zones around Great Britain, France, Italy and in the Eastern Mediterranean:

In the North: The zone is confined by a line at a distance of twenty sea miles along the Dutch coast to Terschelling Lightship, the meridian of longitude from Terschelling Lightship to Udsire; a line from there across the point 62 degrees north, 0 degrees longitude, to 62 degrees north, 5 degrees west; further to a point three sea miles south of the southern point of the Faroe Islands; from there across a point 62 degrees north, 10 degrees west, to 61 degrees north, 15 degrees west, then 57 degrees north, 20 degrees west, to 47 degrees north, 20 degrees west; further, to 43 degrees north, 15 degrees west; then along the parallel of latitude 43 degrees north to twenty sea miles from Cape Finisterre, and at a distance of twenty sea miles along the north coast of Spain to the French boundary.

In the South—The Mediterranean: For neutral ships, remains open the sea west of the line Pt. Des Espiquettes to 38 degrees 20 minutes north and 6 degrees east; also north and west of a zone sixty sea miles wide along the North African coast, beginning at 2 degrees longitude west. For the connection of this sea zone with Greece there is provided a zone of a width of twenty sea miles north and east of the following line: 38 degrees north and 6 degrees east to 38 degrees north and 10 degrees west, to 37 degrees north and 11 degrees 30 minutes east, to 34 degrees north and 22 degrees 30 minutes east. From there leads a zone twenty sea miles wide, west of 22 degrees 30 minutes eastern longitude, into Greek territorial waters.

Neutral ships navigating these blockade zones do so at their own risk. Although care has been taken that neutral ships which are on their way toward ports of the blockade zones on February 1, 1917, and have come in the vicinity of the latter, will be spared during a sufficiently long period, it is strongly advised to warn them with all available means in order to cause their return.

Neutral ships which on February 1st are in ports of the blockade zones can with the same safety leave them.

The instructions given to the commanders of German submarines provide for a sufficiently long period during which the safety of passengers on unarmed enemy passenger ships is guaranteed.

Americans en route to the blockade zone on enemy freight steamers are not endangered, as the enemy shipping firms can prevent such ships in time from entering the zone.

Sailing of regular American passenger steamers may continue undisturbed after February 1, 1917, if

(A) The port of destination is Falmouth.

(B) Sailing to or coming from that port course is taken via the Scilly Islands and a point 50 degrees north, 20 degrees west.

(C) The steamers are marked in the following way, which must not be allowed to other vessels in American ports: On ship's hull and superstructure three vertical stripes one meter wide, each to be painted alternately white and red. Each mast should show a large flag checkered white and red, and the stern the American national flag. Care should be taken that, during dark, national flag and painted marks are easily recognizable from a distance, and that the boats are well lighted throughout.

(D) One steamer a week sails in each direction with arrival at Falmouth on Sunday and departure from Falmouth on Wednesday.

(E) United States Government guarantees that no contraband (according to German contraband list) is carried by those steamers.

[For the second Bernstorff memorandum see President Wilson's address, which follows.]

The Imperial German Government on the 31st day of January announced to this Government and to the Governments of the other neutral nations that on and after the 1st day of February, the present month, it would adopt a policy with regard to the use of submarines against all shipping seeking to pass through certain designated areas of the high seas, to which it is clearly my duty to call your attention.

Let me remind the Congress that on the 18th of April last, in view of the sinking on the 24th of March of the cross-channel steamship *Sussex* by a German submarine without summons or warning, and the consequent loss of lives of several citizens of the United States who were passengers aboard her, this Government addressed a note to the Imperial German Government, in which it made the following declaration:

"If it is still the purpose of the Imperial German Government to prosecute relentless and indiscriminate warfare against vessels of commerce by the use of submarines without regard to what the Government of the United States must consider the sacred and indisputable rules of international law and the universally recognized dictates of humanity, the Government of the United States is at last forced to the conclusion that there is but one course it can pursue. Unless the Imperial Government should now immediately declare and effect an abandonment of its present methods of submarine warfare against passenger and freight carrying vessels, the Government of the United States can have no choice but to sever diplomatic relations with the German Empire altogether."

In reply to this declaration the Imperial German Government gave this Government the following assurance:

"The German Government is prepared to do its utmost to confine the operations of war for the rest of its duration to the fighting forces of the belligerents, thereby also insuring the freedom of the seas, a principle upon which the German Government believes now, as before, to be in agreement with the Government of the United States.

"The German Government, guided by this idea, notifies the Government of the United States that the German naval forces have received the following orders: In accordance with the general principles of visit and search and destruction of merchant vessels recognized by international law, such vessels, both within and without the area declared a naval war zone, shall not be sunk without warning and without saving human lives, unless these ships attempt to escape or offer resistance.

"But," it added, "neutrals cannot expect that Germany, forced

TO A MAN

SEVERANCE OF RELATIONS WITH GERMANY

to fight for her existence, shall, for the sake of neutral interest, restrict the use of an effective weapon if her enemy is permitted to continue to apply at will methods of warfare violating the rules of international law. Such a demand would be incompatible with the character of neutrality, and the German Government is convinced that the Government of the United States does not think of making such a demand, knowing that the Government of the United States has repeatedly declared that it is determined to restore the principle of the freedom of the seas, from whatever quarter it has been violated."

To this the Government of the United States replied on the 8th of May, accepting, of course, the assurance given, but adding:

"The Government of the United States feels it necessary to state that it takes it for granted that the Imperial German Government does not intend to imply that the maintenance of its newly announced policy is in any way contingent upon the course or result of diplomatic negotiations between the Government of the United States and any other belligerent Government, notwithstanding the fact that certain passages in the Imperial Government's note of the 4th inst. might appear to be susceptible of that construction. In order, however, to avoid any misunderstanding, the Government of the United States notifies the Imperial Government that it cannot for a moment entertain, much less discuss, a suggestion that respect by German naval authorities for the rights of citizens of the United States upon the high seas should in any way or in the slightest degree be made contingent upon the conduct of any other Government, affecting the rights of neutrals and noncombatants. Responsibility in such matters is single, not joint, absolute, not relative."

To this note of the 8th of May the Imperial German Government made no reply.

On the 31st of January, the Wednesday of the present week, the German Ambassador handed to the Secretary of State, along with a formal note, a memorandum which contained the following statement:

"The Imperial Government therefore does not doubt that the Government of the United States will understand the situation thus forced upon Germany by the Entente Allies' brutal methods of war and by their determination to destroy the Central Powers, and that the Government of the United States will further realize that the now openly disclosed intention of the Entente Allies gives back to Germany the freedom of action which she reserved in her note addressed to the Government of the United States on May 4, 1916.

"Under these circumstances, Germany will meet the illegal measures of her enemies by forcibly preventing, after February 1, 1917, in a zone around Great Britain, France, Italy and in the Eastern Mediterranean, all navigation, that of neutrals included, from and to England and from and to France, etc. All ships met within the zone will be sunk."

I think that you will agree with me that, in view of this declaration, which suddenly and without prior intimation of any kind deliberately withdraws the solemn assurance given in the Imperial Government's note of the 4th of May, 1916, this Government has no alternative consistent with the dignity and honor of the United States but to take the course which, in its note of the 18th of April, 1916, it announced that it would take in the event that the German Government did not declare and effect an abandonment of the methods of submarine warfare which it was then employing and to which it now purposes again to resort.

I have therefore directed the Secretary of State to announce to his Excellency the German Ambassador that all diplomatic relations between the United States and the German Empire are severed and that the American Ambassador to Berlin will immediately be withdrawn; and, in accordance with this decision, to hand to his Excellency his passports.

Notwithstanding this unexpected action of the German Government, this sudden and deplorable renunciation of its assurances, given this Government at one of the most critical moments of tension in the relations of the two Governments, I refuse to believe that it is the intention of the German authorities to do in fact what they have warned us they will feel at liberty to do. I cannot bring myself to believe that they will indeed pay no regard to the ancient friendship between their people and our own or to the solemn obligations which have been exchanged between them, and destroy American ships, and take the lives of American citizens in the willful prosecution of the ruthless naval program they have announced their intention to adopt. Only actual overt acts on their part can make me believe it even now.

If this inveterate confidence on my part in the sobriety and prudent foresight of their purpose should unhappily prove unfounded: if American ships and American lives should in fact be sacrificed by their naval commanders in heedless contravention of the just and reasonable understandings of international law and the obvious dictates of humanity, I shall take the liberty of coming again before the Congress to ask that authority be given me to use any means that may be necessary for the protection of our seamen and our people in the prosecution of their peaceful and legitimate errands on the high seas. I can do nothing less. I take it for granted that all neutral Governments will take the same course.

We do not desire any hostile conflict with the Imperial German Government. We are the sincere friends of the German people, and earnestly desire to remain at peace with the Government which speaks for them. We shall not believe that they are hostile to us unless and until we are obliged to believe it; and we purpose nothing more than the reasonable defense of the undoubted rights of our people. We wish to serve no selfish ends. We seek merely to stand true alike in thought and in action to the immemorial principles of our people, which I have sought to express in my address to the Senate only two weeks ago—seek merely to vindicate our right to liberty and justice and an unmolested life. These are the bases of peace, not war. God grant that we may not be challenged to defend them by acts of willful injustice on the part of the Government of Germany!

"All the News That's Fit to Print."

The New York Times.

THE WEATHER
Probably snow or rain today and Friday; wind northeast.
For full weather report see Page 21.

VOL. LXVI...NO. 21,586.

NEW YORK, THURSDAY, MARCH 1, 1917.—TWENTY-TWO PAGES.

ONE CENT In Greater New York. | TWO CENTS In New England and Middle States.

GERMANY SEEKS AN ALLIANCE AGAINST US; ASKS JAPAN AND MEXICO TO JOIN HER; FULL TEXT OF HER PROPOSAL MADE PUBLIC

[CONG]RESS TO BACK WILSON

[La]conia Tragedy Adds Strength to President's Support.

[MO]DIFIED BILL IN HOUSE

Leaders Predict That Senate's Armed Neutrality Measure Will Prevail.

[THI]NK PUBLIC IS AROUSED

[De]tention of Five Consuls in [Ger]many Increases Crisis— [New] Demand on Turkey.

[Pres]ident Insists on Passage of Senate Armed Ship Bill

Special to The New York Times.
WASHINGTON, Feb. 28.—Opposition to granting authority to the President to protect American lives and trade at sea began melting away and Administration leaders quietly predicted action within another twenty-four hours.

No Ships Sunk Yesterday; 456,817 Tons Lost in February

No new sinkings by German submarines were reported yesterday. A record of the tonnage sunk in the German blockade zone during the whole month of February, compiled from British Admiralty figures and papers received from other sources, follows:

NUMBER OF SHIPS SUNK.

British	81	110
Other	2	20

TOTAL TONNAGE DESTROYED.

British	35,869	216,304
Other		

Grand total : (Feb. 1-28,) 456,817 tons.

WILSON GIVES OUT APPEAL FROM HOY

American Whose Mother and Sister Died on the Laconia Asks That They Be Avenged.

OFFERS SERVICES TO NATION

Young, Nephew of Mrs. Hoy, Appeals to Wilson, Lansing, Wadsworth, and Chandler.

Zimmermann Says Again Neutral Ships Will Be Sunk; Escape of the Orleans Only an Instance of Luck

Special Cable to The New York Times.
BERLIN, Feb. 28. (via London.)—The report of the safe arrival of the freighter Orleans at Bordeaux did not cause much surprise here, as it was known that there were heavy fogs along the course most likely to be selected by the American vessel, which would naturally render the operations of the U-boats extremely difficult.

BERLIN TO REPLACE SEVEN DUTCH SHIPS

Offers Freighters for Vessels Sunk, but Holland Must Buy Them After War.

MOTIVE BEHIND SINKINGS

Hint in Washington That Berlin Ordered Destruction of Ships to Settle Holland's Policy.

GERMANY HOLDS FIVE U.S. CONSULS

Held Because a Teuton Was Detained in Cuba—Their Release Now Asked.

RITTER UNDER SUSPICION

Officials Think Swiss Legation Leaked in Detaining of Consuls and Yarrowdale Note.

JAPAN CALLS IT MONSTROUS

Embassy Issues Statement Scouting Germany's Proposal.

RELATIONS WITH US CLOSER

Tokio Gratified by Abandonment of Exclusion Bills in Oregon and Idaho.

FLOOD SURE OF CONGRESS

Representative Says Revelation Will Insure Backing of President for Defense Preparation.

Text of Germany's Proposal to Form an Alliance With Mexico and Japan Against the United States

[Supplied by the Associated Press as an authentic copy of the German Foreign Minister's note to the German Minister in Mexico.]

BERLIN, Jan. 19, 1917.

On the 1st of February we intend to begin submarine warfare unrestricted. In spite of this, it is our intention to endeavor to keep neutral the United States of America.

If this attempt is not successful, we propose an alliance on the following basis with Mexico: That we shall make war together and together make peace. We shall give general financial support, and it is understood that Mexico is to reconquer the lost territory in New Mexico, Texas, and Arizona. The details are left to you for settlement.

You are instructed to inform the President of Mexico of the above in the greatest confidence as soon as it is certain that there will be an outbreak of war with the United States, and suggest that the President of Mexico, on his own initiative, should communicate with Japan suggesting adherence at once to this plan. At the same time, offer to mediate between Germany and Japan.

Please call to the attention of the President of Mexico that the employment of ruthless submarine warfare now promises to compel England to make peace in a few months.

ZIMMERMANN.

FILIBUSTER FOR EXTRA SESSION

Senate Republicans Force Interminable Roll Calls on Amendments to Revenue Bill.

BILL PASSED, 47 TO 33

PACIFISTS PRESS VIEWS ON WILSON

Bryan, Jane Addams, and Others in Two Groups Confer with the President.

FEAR DECLARATION OF WAR

WASHINGTON EXPO[SES]

Our Governme[nt] [Knew of] Zimmermann['s Note] of Jan. [19]

BIG PROMISES [MADE]

Conquest of Texas, [New Mex]ico, and Arizon[a Held] Out as a Lure [to Mexico]

BERNSTORFF CHI[EF PLOTTER]

German Embassy [in Washing]ton Head Centre[d In]trigues in This Ho[stile Plan]

C. "The Zimmermann Telegram,"
Dr. Alfred Zimmermann's secret note to
Germany's Minister to Mexico, Heinrich Von Eckhardt

BERLIN, January 19, 1917

On the first of February we intend to begin submarine warfare unrestricted. In spite of this it is our intention to endeavor to keep neutral the United States of America.

If this attempt is not successful, we propose an alliance on the following basis with Mexico:

That we shall make war together and together make peace. We shall give general financial support and it is understood that Mexico is to reconquer the lost territory in New Mexico, Texas and Arizona. The details are left to you for settlement.

You are instructed to inform the President of Mexico of the above in the greatest confidence as soon as it is certain that there will be an outbreak of war with the United States, and suggest that the President of Mexico, on his own initiative, should communicate with Japan suggesting adherence at once to this plan; at the same time offer to mediate between Germany and Japan.

Please call to the attention of the President of Mexico that the employment of ruthless submarine warfare now promises to compel England to make peace in a few months.

(Signed) Zimmermann.

GENTLEMEN OF THE CONGRESS:

I have called the Congress into extraordinary session because there are serious, very serious choices of policy to be made, and made immediately, which it was neither right nor constitutionally permissible that I should assume the responsibility of making.

On the third of February last I officially laid before you the extraordinary announcement of the Imperial German Government that on and after the first day of February it was its purpose to put aside all restraints of law or of humanity and use its submarines to sink every vessel that sought to approach either the ports of Great Britain and Ireland or the western coasts of Europe or any of the ports controlled by the enemies of Germany within the Mediterranean. That had seemed to be the object of the German submarine warfare earlier in the war, but since April of last year the Imperial Government had somewhat restrained the commanders of its undersea craft in conformity with its promise then given to us that passenger boats should not be sunk and that due warning would be given to all other vessels which its submarines might seek to destroy, when no resistance was offered or escape attempted, and care taken that their crews were given at least a fair chance to save their lives in their open boats. The precautions taken were meager and haphazard enough, as was proved in distressing instance after instance in the progress of the cruel and unmanly business, but a certain degree of restraint was observed. The new policy has swept every restriction aside. Vessels of every kind, whatever their flag, their character, their cargo, their destination, their errand, have been ruthlessly sent to the bottom without warning and without thought of help or mercy for those on board, the vessels of friendly neutrals along with those of belligerents. Even hospital ships and ships carrying relief to the sorely bereaved and stricken people of Belgium, though the latter were provided with safe conduct through the proscribed areas by the German Government itself and were distinguished by unmistakable marks of identity, have been sunk with the same reckless lack of compassion or of principle.

The New Dictator

I was for a little while unable to believe that such things would in fact be done by any Government that had hitherto subscribed to humane practices of civilized nations. International law had its origin in the attempt to set up some law which would be respected and observed upon the seas, where no nation had right of dominion and where lay the free highways of the world. By painful stage after stage has that law been built up, with meager enough results, indeed, after all was accomplished that could be accomplished, but always with a clear view, at least, of what the heart and conscience of mankind demanded. This minimum of right the German Government has swept aside, under the plea of retaliation and necessity and because it had no weapons which it could use at sea except these which it is impossible to employ as it is employing them without throwing to the wind all scruples of humanity or of respect for the understandings that were supposed to underlie the intercourse of the world. I am not now thinking of the loss of property involved, immense and serious as that is, but only of the wanton and wholesale destruction of the lives of noncombatants, men, women and children, engaged in pursuits which have always, even in the darkest periods of modern history, been deemed innocent and legitimate. Property can be paid for; the lives of peaceful and innocent people cannot be. The present German submarine warfare against commerce is a warfare against mankind.

It is a war against all nations. American ships have been sunk, American lives taken, in ways which it has stirred us very deeply to learn of, but the ships and people of other neutral and friendly nations have been sunk and overwhelmed in the waters in the same way. There has been no discrimination. The challenge is to all mankind. Each nation must decide for itself how it will meet it. The choice we make for ourselves must be made with a moderation of counsel and a temperateness of judgment befitting our character and our motives as a nation. We must put excited feeling away. Our motive will not be revenge or the victorious assertion of the physical might of the nation, but only the vindication of right, of human right, of which we are only a single champion.

When I addressed the Congress on the twenty-sixth of February last I thought that it would suffice to assert our neutral rights with arms, our right to use the seas against unlawful interference, our right to keep our people safe against unlawful violence. But armed neutrality, it now appears, is impracticable. Because submarines are in effect outlaws when used as the German submarines have been used against merchant shipping, it is impossible to defend ships against their attacks as the law of nations has assumed that merchantmen would defend themselves against privateers or cruisers, visible craft giving chase upon the open sea. It is common prudence in such circumstances, grim necessity indeed, to endeavor to destroy them before they have shown their own intention. They must be dealt with upon sight, if dealt with at all. The German Government denies the right of neutrals to use arms at all within the areas of the sea which it has proscribed, even in the defense of rights which no modern publicist has ever before questioned their right to defend. The intimation is conveyed that the armed guards which we have placed on our merchant ships will be treated as beyond the pale of law and subject to be dealt with as pirates would be. Armed neutrality is ineffectual enough at best; in such circumstances and in the face of such pretensions it is worse than ineffectual; it is likely only to produce what it was meant to prevent; it is practically certain to draw us into the war without either the rights or the effectiveness of belligerents. There is one choice we cannot make, we are incapable of making; we will not choose the path of submission and suffer the most sacred rights of our nation and our people to be ignored or violated. The wrongs against which we now array ourselves are no common wrongs; they cut to the very roots of human life.

With a profound sense of the solemn and even tragical character of the step I am taking and of the grave responsibilities which it involves, but in unhesitating obedience to what I deem my constitutional duty, I advise that the Congress declare the recent course of the Imperial German Government to be in fact nothing less than war against the Government and people of the United States; that it formally accept the status of belligerent which has thus been thrust upon it; and that it take immediate steps not only to put the country in a more thorough state of defense, but also to exert all its power and employ all its resources to bring the Government of the German Empire to terms and end the war.

What this will involve is clear. It will involve the utmost practicable cooperation in counsel and action with the governments now at war with Germany, and, as incident to that, the extension to those governments of the most liberal financial credits, in order that our resources may so far as possible be added to theirs. It will involve the organization and mobilization of all the material resources of the country to supply the materials of war and serve the incidental needs of the nation in the most abundant and yet the most economical and efficient way possible. It will involve the immediate full equipment of the navy in all respects but particularly in supplying it with the best means of dealing with the enemy's submarines. It will involve the immediate addition to the armed forces of the United States already provided for by law in case of war of at least five hundred thousand men, who should, in my opinion, be chosen upon the principle of universal liability to service, and also the authorization of subsequent additional increments of equal force so soon as they may be needed and can be handled in training. It will involve also, of course, the granting of adequate credits to the Government, sustained, I hope, so far as they can equitably be sustained by the present generation, by well-conceived taxation.

I say sustained so far as may be equitable by taxation because it seems to me that it would be most unwise to base the credits which will now be necessary entirely on money borrowed. It is our duty, I most respectfully urge, to protect our people so far as we may against the very serious hardships and evils which would be likely to arise out of the inflation which would be produced by vast loans.

In carrying out the measures by which these things are to be accomplished we should keep constantly in mind the wisdom of interfering as little as possible in our own preparations and in the equipment of our own military forces with the duty—for it will be a very practical duty—of supplying the nations already at war with Germany with the materials which they can obtain only from us or by our assistance. They are in the field and we should help them in every way to be effective there.

I shall take the liberty of suggesting, through the several executive departments of the Government, for the consideration of your committees, measures for the accomplishment of the several objects I have mentioned. I hope that it will be your pleasure to deal with them as having been framed after very careful thought by the branch of the Government upon whom the responsibility of conducting the war and safeguarding the nation will most directly fall.

While we do these things, these deeply momentous things, let us be very clear, and make very clear to all the world, what our motives and our objects are. My own thought has not been driven from its habitual and normal course by the unhappy events of the last two months, and I do not believe that the thought of the nation has been altered or clouded by them. I have exactly the same things in mind now that I had in mind when I addressed the Senate on the twenty-second of January last; the same that I had in mind when I addressed the Congress on the third of February and on the twenty-sixth of February. Our object now, as then, is to vindicate the principles of peace and justice in the life of the world as against selfish and autocratic power, and to set up among the really free and self-governed peoples of the world such a concert of purpose and of action as will henceforth insure the observance of those principles. Neutrality is no longer feasible or desirable where the peace of the world is involved and the freedom of its peoples, and the menace to that peace and freedom lies in the existence of autocratic governments, backed by organized force which is controlled wholly by their will, not by the will of their people. We have seen the last of neutrality in such circumstances. We are at the beginning of an age in which it will be insisted that the same standards of conduct and of responsibility for wrong done shall be observed among nations and their governments that are observed among the individual citizens of civilized States.

We have no quarrel with the German people. We have no feeling towards them but one of sympathy and friendship. It was not upon their impulse that their government acted in entering this war. It was not with their previous knowledge or approval. It was a war determined upon as wars used to be determined upon in the old, unhappy days when peoples were nowhere consulted by their rulers and wars were provoked and waged in the interest of dynasties or of little groups of ambitious men who were accustomed to use their fellowmen as pawns and tools. Self-governed nations do not fill their neighbor states with spies or set the course of intrigue to bring about some critical posture of affairs which will give them an opportunity to strike and make conquest. Such designs can be successfully worked out only under cover and where no one has the right to ask questions. Cunningly contrived plans of deception or agression, carried, it may be, from generation to generation, can be worked out and kept from the light only within the privacy of courts or behind the carefully guarded confidences of a narrow and privileged class. They are happily impossible where public opinion commands and insists upon full information concerning all the nation's affairs.

A steadfast concert for peace can never be maintained except by a partnership of democratic nations. No autocratic government could be trusted to keep faith within it or observe its covenants. It must be a league of honor, a partnership of opinion. Intrigue would eat its vitals away; the plottings of inner circles who could plan what they would and render account to no one would be a corruption seated at its very heart. Only free peoples can hold their purpose and their honor steady to a common end and prefer the interests of mankind to any narrow interest of their own.

Does not every American feel that assurance has been added to our hope for the future peace of the world by the wonderful and heartening things that have been happening within the last few weeks in Russia? Russia was known by those who knew her best to have been always in fact democratic at heart, in all the vital habits of her thought, in all the intimate relationships of her people that spoke their natural instinct, their habitual attitude toward life. The autocracy that crowned the summit of her political structure, long as it had stood and terrible as was the reality of its power, was not in fact Russian in origin, character, or purpose; and now it has been shaken off and the great, generous Russian people have been added, in all their naive majesty and might, to the forces that are fighting for freedom in the world, for justice, and for peace. Here is a fit partner for a League of Honor.

One of the things that has served to convince us that the Prussian autocracy was not and could never be our friend is that from the very outset of the present war it has filled our unsuspecting communities, and even our offices of government, with spies and set criminal intrigues everywhere afoot against our national unity of counsel, our peace within and without, our industries and our commerce. Indeed, it is now evident that its spies were here even before the war began; and it is unhappily not a matter of conjecture but a fact proved in our courts of justice that the intrigues which have more than once come perilously near to disturbing the peace and dislocating the industries of the country have been carried on at the instigation, with the support, and even under the personal direction of official agents of the Imperial Government accredited to the Government of the United States. Even in checking these things and trying to extirpate them we have sought to put the most generous interpretation possible upon them because we knew that their source lay, not in any hostile feeling or purpose of the German people toward us (who were, no doubt, as ignorant of them as we ourselves were), but only in the selfish designs of a Government that did what it pleased and told its people nothing. But they have played their part in serving to convince us at last that that Government entertains no real friendship for us, and means to act against our peace and security at its convenience. That it means to stir up enemies against us at our very doors the intercepted note to the German Minister at Mexico City is eloquent evidence.

We are accepting this challenge of hostile purpose because we know that in such a government, following such methods, we can never have a friend; and that in the presence of its organized power, always lying in wait to accomplish we know not what purpose, there can be no assured security for the democratic governments of the world. We are now about to accept the gauge of battle with this natural foe to liberty and shall, if necessary, spend the whole force of the nation to check and nullify its pretensions and its power. We are glad, now that we see the facts with no veil of false pretense about them, to fight thus for the ultimate peace of the world and for the liberation of its peoples, the German peoples included; for the rights of nations, great and small, and the privilege of men everywhere to choose their way of life and of obedience. The world must be made safe for democracy. Its peace must be planted upon the tested foundations of political liberty. We have no selfish ends to serve. We desire no conquest, no dominion. We seek no indemnities for ourselves, no material compensation for the sacrifices we shall freely make. We are but one of the champions of the rights of mankind. We shall be satisfied when those rights have been made as secure as the faith and the freedom of nations can make them.

Just because we fight without rancor and without selfish object, seeking nothing for ourselves but what we shall wish to share with all free peoples, we shall, I feel confident, conduct our operations as belligerents without passion and ourselves observe with proud punctilio the principles of right and of fair play we profess to be fighting for.

I have said nothing of the governments allied with the Imperial Government of Germany because they have not made war upon us or challenged us to defend our right and our honor. The Austro-Hungarian Government has, indeed, avowed its unqualified endorsement and acceptance of the reckless and lawless submarine warfare adopted now without disguise by the Imperial German Government, and it has therefore not been possible for this Government to receive Count Tarnowski, the Ambassador recently accredited to this Government by the Imperial and Royal Government of Austria-Hungary; but that Government has not actually engaged in warfare against citizens of the

United States on the seas, and I take the liberty, for the present at least, of postponing a discussion of our relations with the authorities at Vienna. We enter this war only where we are clearly forced into it because there are no other means of defending our rights.

It will be all the easier for us to conduct ourselves as belligerents in a high spirit of right and fairness because we act without animus, not with enmity toward a people or with the desire to bring any injury or disadvantage upon them, but only in armed opposition to an irresponsible government which has thrown aside all considerations of humanity and of right and is running amuck. We are, let me say again, the sincere friends of the German people, and shall desire nothing so much as the early reestablishment of intimate relations of mutual advantage between us,—however hard it may be for them, for the time being, to believe that this is spoken from our hearts. We have borne with their present government through all these bitter months because of that friendship, exercising a patience and forbearance which would otherwise have been impossible. We shall, happily, still have an opportunity to prove that friendship in our daily attitude and actions toward the millions of men and women of German birth and native sympathy who live among us and share our life, and we shall be proud to prove it towards all who are in fact loyal to their neighbors and to the Government in the hour of test. They are, most of them, as true and loyal Americans as if they had never known any other fealty or allegiance. They will be prompt to stand with us in rebuking and restraining the few who may be of a different mind and purpose. If there should be disloyalty, it will be dealt with with a firm hand of stern repression; but, if it lifts its head at all, it will lift it only here and there and without countenance except from a lawless and malignant few.

It is a distressing and oppressive duty, Gentlemen of the Congress, which I have performed in thus addressing you. There are, it may be, many months of fiery trial and sacrifice ahead of us. It is a fearful thing to lead this great peaceful people into war, into the most terrible and disastrous of all wars, civilization itself seeming to be in the balance. But the right is more precious than peace, and we shall fight for the things which we have always carried nearest our hearts—for democracy, for the right of those who submit to authority to have a voice in their own governments, for the rights and liberties of small nations, for a universal dominion of right by such a concert of free peoples as shall bring peace and safety to all nations and make the world itself at last free. To such a task we can dedicate our lives and our fortunes, everything that we are and everything that we have, with the pride of those who know that the day has come when America is privileged to spend her blood and her might for the principles that gave her birth and happiness and the peace which she has treasured. God helping her, she can do no other.

Front!

Clerk: "There is a lady just leaving.   You may have her room."

E. United States Declaration of War against Germany

Sixty-fifth Congress of the United States of America;

At the First Session

Begun and held at the City of Washington on Monday, the second day of April, one thousand nine hundred and seventeen

Joint Resolution Declaring that a state of war exists between the Imperial German Government and the Government and the people of the United States and making provision to prosecute the same.

Whereas the Imperial German Government has committed repeated acts of war against the Government and the people of the United States of America; Therefore, be it

Resolved by the Senate and House of Representatives of the United States of America in Congress assembled, That the state of war between the United States and the Imperial German Government which has thus been thrust upon the United States is hereby formally declared; and that the President be, and he is hereby, authorized and directed to employ the entire naval and military forces of the United States and the resources of the Government to carry on war against the Imperial German Government; and to bring the conflict to a successful termination all the resources of the country are hereby pledged by the Congress of the United States.

CHAMP CLARK,
Speaker of the House of Representatives

Approved,
April 6, 1917
WOODROW WILSON

THOS. R. MARSHALL,
Vice President of the United States and
President of the Senate.

PICTURE CREDITS

PAGE	SOURCE
1	Library of Congress
2	Chicago *Daily Tribune*
10	Library of Congress
12	Culver Pictures
13	Brown Brothers
14	National Archives
15	National Archives
16-17	National Archives
18	Culver Pictures
19	Culver Pictures
20 Top	National Archives
20 Bottom	National Archives
21	European
22	National Archives
23	European
24 Top	National Archives
24 Bottom	National Archives
25	National Archives
26 Left	National Archives
26 Right	National Archives
27	National Archives
28	National Archives
29	Library of Congress
30	Brown Brothers
31	Culver Pictures
32	Brown Brothers
33	Culver Pictures
35	Brown Brothers
36	Library of Congress
37	Underwood & Underwood
38 Top	National Archives
38 Bottom	National Archives
39	Wide World
40 Top	Underwood & Underwood
40 Bottom	Wide World
41 Left	Brown Brothers
41 Right	Wide World
42 Top	National Archives
42 Bottom	National Archives
43 Top	National Archives
43 Bottom	National Archives
44 Top	Wide World
44 Bottom	Wide World
45	National Archives
49	Brown Brothers
50-51	Wide World
52	European
53	Library of Congress
54	Brown Brothers
55	National Archives
56	National Archives
57	National Archives
58	National Archives
59	European
60	National Archives
61	Library of Congress
62	National Archives
68	The Bettmann Archive
71	Brown Brothers
72	New York *Herald*

Page	Source
74	Library of Congress
75 Top	Wide World
75 Bottom	Wide World
76	National Archives
77	Culver Pictures
78	Library of Congress
84-85	National Archives
87	Library of Congress
88	National Archives
89	National Archives
90	National Archives
91	National Archives
92	National Archives
93	Source requests that no credit be given
94	Brown Brothers
95	National Archives
96	European
97	National Archives
98	National Archives
102	National Archives
104	Library of Congress
105	Brooklyn *Daily Eagle*
106	National Archives
107	Culver Pictures
112	Culver Pictures
113	Brooklyn *Daily Eagle*
114	National Archives
115	Library of Congress
116	New York *Evening Telegram*
117	Library of Congress
118	Brown Brothers
119	Library of Congress
120	Brown Brothers
123	Brown Brothers
124	Brown Brothers
130	Library of Congress
131	National Archives
132	Brooklyn *Daily Eagle*
133	French Embassy
135	Culver Pictures
136	Culver Pictures
138	Library of Congress
139	National Archives
140	Brown Brothers
146	Brown Brothers
147	New York *World*
148	Brown Brothers
149	Brooklyn *Daily Eagle*
150	National Archives
151	National Archives
152	New Orleans *Times-Picayune*
153	The Bettmann Archive
156 Top	National Archives
156 Bottom	National Archives
157	National Archives
158 Bottom Left	The Smithsonian Institution
158 Bottom Right	The Smithsonian Institution
159 Bottom Left	The Smithsonian Institution
159 Bottom Right	The Smithsonian Institution
160	National Archives

PAGE	SOURCE
161	National Archives
163 Bottom Left	Brown Brothers
163 Top Right	National Archives
164 Top	U.S. Army Photograph
164 Bottom	National Archives
165	Library of Congress
166	National Archives
170	Wide World
175	New York *Evening Telegram*
178	Wide World
181	Wide World
188	Wide World